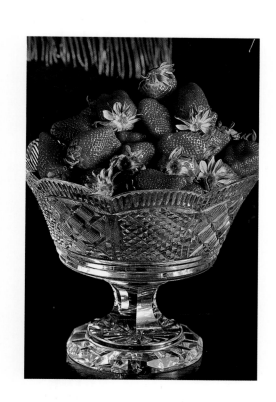

ENTERTAINING
❋❋❋❋❋ *at* *❋❋❋❋❋*
HOME

THE COMPLETE GUIDE TO EVERY
PARTY OCCASION

SHERIDAN ROGERS

with a preface by
Lord Wedgwood of Barlaston

CASSELL

Contents

Preface

Wedgwood has been associated with the art of entertaining since the 1700s and much has changed over that time. Migration, mass transport and the media have opened up our world—and our homes—to the influences of many countries, climates, and cultures. Daily access to a multitude of foods and ingredients gives us more opportunity to develop exciting and creative menus—not to mention how we present them.

In this century alone, a dramatic change has taken place in the way that we live and work. Modern living requires most households that enjoy the art of entertaining to combine the gracious elements established by our ancestors with the practicalities of today's faster pace of life. Although the formal dinner party is far from extinct, we now enjoy entertaining in many different ways. A variety of breakfast styles are available; lunches can be simple but elegant; and we are rediscovering afternoon tea. Barbecues and picnics provide versatility and a change to normal entertaining, and—beyond an assortment of dinners—we find more excuses for celebrations of varying sizes with family and friends at Christmas, anniversaries, and public holidays. That's why Wedgwood comes in a broad range of designs, from traditional to contemporary, to suit individual lifestyles and complement any meal of the day. That's why this book provides not only fourteen very different menus for entertaining but inspiring ideas and hints (not rules) that cover everything from choosing a theme for a meal to a guide to modern etiquette.

The key to successful entertaining, however simple or elaborate, is to combine all the elements relative to your environment or situation and create an occasion that you will enjoy: your guests are more likely to have a good time if you are happy!

Wedgwood continues to concentrate on the quality of its products. Some designs could be considered very traditional, but today most are recognized as timeless classics, including recent introductions. The delicate, translucent beauty of fine bone china holds it own in modern times for the material is surprisingly strong and robust. Its relevance to contemporary entertaining is nowhere more evident than in the pages of this book, where it has been used beautifully in a host of settings from a child's party to a romantic dinner for two.

Wedgwood would like to congratulate the publishers and all those associated with this project for producing an item of beauty and practicality. We are proud of our association with this book which continues the warm tradition of sharing food with family and friends while bringing to it new life and fresh ideas that are applicable to today's way of life. We also applaud its quality and excellence: because we know that by buying the best there is, you are not only assured value but much enjoyment for years to come.

Wedgwood

Lord Wedgwood of Barlaston

Introduction

"The joys of the table belong equally to all ages, conditions, countries and times..."

Brillat-Savarin

Sharing a meal with friends is one of life's greatest pleasures. Real friendships are nurtured in this way, and a home-cooked meal shared with other people is one of the best ways to appease daily stresses and anxieties.

Many years ago, entertaining at home was the major form of entertainment for most people. Then we went through a period when everybody, it seemed, was eating in restaurants or noisy, bright fast-food halls where conversation was minimal and the atmosphere distracting.

Nowadays, people are returning to the sanctity of their homes and inviting family, friends, and associates in. This may have something to do with economics. We not only live in less affluent times, but with the financial and personal commitment many of us have to our houses, it makes sense to spend time enjoying them. Entertaining at home also opens possibilities to make more meaningful contact with people, to meet on a more intimate basis. You have a better feel for another person when you are invited to their home (or when they are invited to yours), a better sense of their tastes, likes and dislikes, what's important to them, even what their values and priorities are. In a restaurant, people are not framed by their background, so you don't see the whole picture. They are often less relaxed, and therefore less revealing about themselves.

Entertaining at home is an art, and like all the arts, requires time and care and attention to detail. It requires a certain "savoir faire" which can be acquired as can the knowledge of the etiquette for certain occasions. What is appropriate at an outdoor barbecue, for example, will not apply to a formal dinner.

Use the occasion of a party or special dinner to apply your imagination. Lighting, music and decoration can transform your home into a dramatic setting, creating the right kind of mood for the occasion. Different fabrics can be used to create different effects: calico can be draped from the ceiling to form the insides of a tent; muslin can be hung across windows to soften and give a romantic effect; tulle can be gathered up and scalloped around tables to create interesting table covers. Vases of fragrant flowers, potpourri, or scented candles can also be used to advantage.

Perhaps you don't wish to be so flamboyant? Entertaining at home doesn't have to mean throwing a large party and being extravagant. Nor does it have to be a formal meal in the dining room. Rather, it can be a very simple affair, such as sharing a big bowl of freshly made spaghetti and some crusty garlic bread with the person from next door— a celebration of the ordinary pleasures of daily life. Or it might mean cooking a comforting meal of roast beef and potatoes followed by apple crumble for friends from out-of-town, the kind of food — and atmosphere — you can't get in restaurants.

Don't be put off by thinking you have to spend a great deal of money. In the chapter "An Impromptu Meal from the Pantry", you can see just how easy it is to create a fresh, tasty meal without spending much at all. With a little imagination and without too much forethought, you can put together delicious dishes with ingredients on hand.

Keep the food fresh and simple. Don't fall into the trap of paying excessive attention to its preparation and presentation. Guests can feel decidedly uncomfortable when food is too elaborate or pretentious and their host hovers around it. Rely on fresh fruits and vegetables in season and regional produce with its own naturally good taste. Most of us have a life outside the kitchen!

Put some thought into the table setting. The ambience you create is just as important as the food and wine you serve. This doesn't require a lot of time or expense, but it does require some reflection of your personal style — and confidence. A decorative bowl of baby vegetables can help set the scene for a casual meal; a line of gourds running down the middle of a table can be a welcome change from a vase of flowers. Unusual ideas such as these can be a talking point for guests and will also make them feel you have gone to some trouble to welcome them.

If it's a large gathering such as a wedding or a cocktail party, start planning well ahead. Keep lists. Once you have worked out who the occasion is for and why you are holding it, figure out your budget, your guest list, the theme (if there is one), the dishes for the meal, and the drinks you will serve. If you wish to keep a tally of how much you have spent, collect all your receipts for food and drink and keep them in separate files (labeled paper bags work well).

The key to successful entertaining on any scale is good planning and organization. You want to be able to relax and enjoy yourself too! This is where the ideas and menus in this book can really help. Remember always though that these are guidelines only. They are presented to inspire you to try something different or to mix and match in a way you hadn't considered before. There may be a napkin fold that captures your imagination, but you'd prefer to use a different style of napkin. One of the menus may appeal to you, but you don't like the dessert. You can substitute a dessert from one of the other menus, or use one of your own.

There are no hard and fast rules about entertaining at home. Ultimately, what you bring to it is all important. Experiment and have fun. It is your personal stamp that will make all the difference.

A guide to modern etiquette

We live in a time when the spirit rather than the letter of the laws of etiquette is understood to be what matters. When I'm entertaining at home, above all, I want my guests to feel at ease. For me, that's the essence of hospitality.

Planning and preparation

The etiquette of entertaining at home begins long before the guests arrive. It begins with planning, with composing a guest list. For some occasions, perhaps an engagement party or a business dinner, there'll be some "must ask" people. If the choice of guests is yours alone, aim to assemble a group of people who are likely to enjoy each other. The smaller the guest list, the more important that is. When two guests in a group of six take a dislike to one another, neither the protagonists nor others can escape into a crowded room.

And do consider whether, if all the guests accept, you have enough space for them. For instance, a wedding might have special requirements such as somewhere to cut the cake, a suitable place for photography, room for dancing as well as eating. A cocktail party of cheery guests perched on the arms of chairs and propping up doorways for a couple of hours is one thing. A prolonged crush where people suffer spills and bumps, can't find a seat at supper time nor hear themselves or anyone else talk at conversational decibels, is something else.

You'll see from the recipes in this book that my preference when entertaining is for fresh food, balanced between rich and light, offering a variety of types and textures, and as easy for guests to manage as it is for hosts to prepare and serve.

Ask guests beforehand if they have special dietary requirements. This is quite easily done with informal, particularly telephone, invitations. It's virtually impossible with formal ones. Consider the possiblity of one or more guests being vegetarian, Jewish, or Muslim, or eating white-meat only. To be safe, you could plan so that at least one of the first two courses would cater for their tastes. In this way, a guest may be given a further portion of a vegetarian first course, for example, with the normal vegetable side dishes or salads, while others are served the second course. What to do if a course is unsuitable for a guest? Without fussing, try to rustle up some food acceptable to them (an omelette is a great standby). If you can't find something suitable, the only thing to do is to express your regret.

Invitations

No matter how formal or informal, whether handwritten, custom-printed, or readymade, delivered by mail, fax, or telephone, every invitation should include the basics. The first of these is to make clear who is the host (you alone or with someone else). Secondly, specify who is invited. Adults only, or children as well? Thirdly, describe the kind of event you're hosting, be it lunch, a christening, or a bar mitzvah. Next, if you're celebrating a special occasion, mention that graduation, anniversary, or religious festival. At this point, explain if the occasion is to celebrate a particular person or their achievement.

Then name the day, the date, and the hour (before or after midday) when the event will take place. If you're giving a cocktail party, you might include a finishing time so you don't find yourself feeding brunch to a few die-hard guests the next day. For dinner parties, 8 pm for 8.30 pm means that guests are invited to arrive from 8 pm and that you'll be serving the meal at 8.30 pm. Last but not least, the invitation should clearly state where your guests are to present themselves (your address, or your co-host's, perhaps).

It's a courtesy to let people know if an occasion has a particular theme, requires fancy dress, is casual, informal, or formal. If you plan to wear jeans, tell your guests. If they're in the mood to wear their tiaras when the time comes, that's their choice. But never ever be the kind of host who says, "Oh, I'll be wearing my jeans", and then greets guests resplendent in her own tiara.

Some hosts add simply "Regrets Only", rather than RSVP, the acronym for the French respondez s'il vous plait ("please reply"). If they don't hear to the contrary, they assume acceptance. I tried the "Regrets Only" option once. But the thought that I wouldn't know if the invitations had been received was driving me crazy, so I had to call all the guests to save my sanity. At least with the RSVP system, I need to call only those who don't respond.

The best a host can do is allow people ample time to respond to invitations. Custom has it that a host should mail invitations to formal occasions four to six weeks before the date. Mail, telephone, or fax invitations to informal events ten days to three weeks ahead of time. Some people like to follow telephone invitations and acceptances with reminder cards or notes.

But were spontaneity ever ruled offensive, it would be a sad day for guests and hosts alike. One of the nicest invitations anyone can get is a telephone call or handwritten note saying "This is very short notice, but we'd like you to come to (lunch, dinner, drinks or whatever) at such and such a time (being anywhere from a mere one to seven days in advance)." If you need someone to help you fill the social gaps you're sure will loom when guests have dropped out of a small dinner party at the last moment, why not appeal to an understanding friend? If you'd be pleased to help them out in similar circumstances, chances are that they are like-minded.

Ready-made invitations are perfectly acceptable, while handwritten ones are always charming. You can employ modern scribes to pen them, but if it's a large guest list, consider conscripting family members and friends with legible handwriting. When you're ordering custom-printed invitations, the printer should have a range of samples to help you devise something attractive. It's hard to go wrong if you keep it simple when choosing stationery or typeface.

These tried-and-true guidelines apply equally to formal or informal invitations. But with informal invitations, there's more room for individuality and ingenuity to create objects of visual delight, statements of wit and festivity as well as fact.

If your house is hard to find, accompany your invitations with a note in the form of a map, public transport details for non-drivers, and the telephone number in case your guests get lost anyway. If parking can be a problem, advise your guests in advance. For me, the hard-to-find category includes houses with no street numbers or exterior lights, broken pathways strewn with toys or gardening gear, or strung with spiderwebs. Do make sure the approach to your front door is not an obstacle course.

Welcoming your guests

After greeting your guests, it's considerate to offer them somewhere to leave their belongings and a chance to "brush up" before offering them a drink and introducing them to others.

As they arrive, some guests may present you with fresh flowers, chocolates, a bottle of wine, or perhaps all three. If it's convenient, put the flowers in water in any handy vessel, even the bath. Rarely will you have time to hunt around for the right vase and fiddle with flowers. If it is a casual gathering, your guests may enjoy chatting with you while you arrange the flowers and then seeing their gift on display. Similiarly, it is usual for food and wine to be shared with the guests, if suitable, as their contribution to the occasion, but this is not necessarily the rule. Rely on your guests to expect you to have catered for their every need.

In case everyone arrives simultaneously, it's sensible to have a drinks tray prepared for your guests to help themselves instead of waiting until you have cleared the tangle of people at the front door. If there is more than one person hosting the occasion, one can do the welcoming and another the drinks and introductions. Solo hosts can opt to rely on one or two well-briefed guests to play the role of drinks waiter and make the introductions.

Introductions

The best introduction is a clearly spoken, individual name. Avoid potted biographies when making introductions. If you'd like to give your guests a conversation-starter, keep it simple. "John Samestreet, who lives next door" or "Polly Perfect, our houseguest" are fine. The names-only technique also avoids the possibility of any social awkwardness in relation to same-sex couples, de facto couples, husbands or wives and their lovers, or those who may be offended by being defined by a relationship. Many married women now prefer to be known by their birth or chosen name and not their husband's. Others use both, one professionally and one socially. It's worth checking to avoid giving offense.

Customarily, men are introduced to women: "Jill, meet Jack. Jack, this is Jill." And, again abiding by tradition, younger people are introduced to older people. These days, however, when equality outweighs ceremonial deference, few are inclined to be offended if you depart from the traditional mode.

No one enjoys coming into a room and being introduced to a crowd, although sometimes it can't be helped. Hearing a dozen or more names rattled off by a host seems to mesmerize me so that my memory completely shuts down. Try to avoid this situation. When possible, it's considerate to give them some idea in advance about the size and composition of your party, but a quick, quiet word with them on their arrival may be all that is possible.

And what should you do if, as you go to introduce people you know well, their names escape you? Say something honest like: "This is awful. My mind's a blank. Quickly, your names!" or dissemble with "You know each other, of course!" and trust them to rescue you. Don't flay yourself over such things. Hosts don't have to be perfect.

Some guests need help to socialize. Introduce them to one or two people at a time, keep a discreet eye on how they're coping, and look for an opportunity to introduce them to others soon. The best hosts ensure that, at smaller parties at least, everyone meets everyone else.

Dinner party etiquette

Sharing food, that classic symbol of friendship, is central to entertaining at home. I relish the fact that the word "companion" echoes the Latin for "with" and "bread". And in our socially relaxed times, whatever the occasion, customs concerning seating, serving, eating, and conversation are all based in common sense and consideration. The dinner party, at its best, can be a perfect microcosm of modern etiquette—the practise of thoughtful graces without airs.

The meal is usually served somewhere between 7:30 pm and 9 pm, with guests invited to arrive from half an hour before and expected to stay for about three hours altogether. Most working people can arrange to present themselves in the evenings by that hour, but if it suits to move the meal forward or back, feel free.

When people are running late, and there's a risk of something spoiling in the kitchen, or other guests are getting ravenous or feeling the effects of alcohol, start dining rather than wait for the latecomers. That way they'll be mortified only by being unpunctual, not by ruining everyone's dinner.

Before dinner, as at a cocktail party, make sure your guests have somewhere safe to place a drink, and that you have suitably protected your furniture. Provide plenty of small napkins for dealing with the nibbles. Don't replenish people's drinks without asking them, nor fill glasses so full that it's easy to spill the contents. If there are any accidents, minimize your guest's embarrassment by cleaning up as well and as quickly as you can without making a fuss.

Seating plans

A friend of mine likes to reminisce about "the nights of the round table", referring to a time when we shared an apartment with a wonderful, circular dining table that ensured no one was ever left in the conversational cold. Our next table was rectangular. Parties of six presented no difficulties, but with eight we learned that the most socially effective seating plan placed the two liveliest guests in the middle at each side and opposite each other.

We didn't bother with place cards then, and with small numbers, I don't now. With larger numbers, or more than one table, I do. Hosts can't be everywhere at once and it's tedious for guests to hover around—or worse, to move from one placing to another—while waiting to be allocated a seat. Some hosts address this problem by using a seating list.

For informal dinners, or formal dinners with family and close friends, first names only should be written on the cards. If you have children, they may like to do this. If appropriate, they can also help with serving food and drink, make introductions and conversation—enjoying their contribution and learning the skills that will make them excellent hosts themselves.

When doing the place cards, match the tone of more formal dinners by using both names on cards placed behind the individual settings. For less formal affairs, it is fine to use first names only and a second initial if two guests share the same name. But formal or informal, it's courteous to ensure you spell people's names correctly.

An excellent seating plan is one where people enjoy the company of those around them and bring out the best in each other as guests. There is no longer concern about inviting a 50-50 gender mix to maintain the tradition of seating men and women alternately, nor about placing married or unmarried couples apart. Nor does giving a guest of honor the best place mean the one at your right hand if you'll be up and down from the table supervizing the progress of the meal. Instead, place them directly opposite you, or between two people whom you think the special guest will especially enjoy.

Serving food and drinks

You will probably need someone to help you serve at table during a formal dinner party with more than four or five guests. When numbers exceed 12, unless you wish to hire waiters, it would be better to organize a "seated buffet". People serve themselves from platters presented on a sideboard or a kitchen bench—somewhere accessible to guests and to one or more dinner tables set with glassware, china, cutlery, candles, and flowers where people can then be seated.

Another option when both kitchen and dining space is at a premium is for a course to be served directly onto each guest's plate in the kitchen then delivered immediately to the seated guests.

If you do engage casual staff, extend your courtesy to them also. Before the occasion, explain precisely the assistance you want and how you'd like them to dress, and agree on fees. Be sure you introduce the staff to all those involved with hosting the event and to the person to be served first, the guest of honor. And nothing's more embarrassing for guests than to see their host being terse or patronizing with employees.

It doesn't really work for anyone other than a permanently employed professional butler to seriously announce that "dinner is served". At best, it's a tired joke. A confident host asks guests to come to dinner and leads the way to the buffet or table. With larger numbers, ask one or two of your guests to lead others to dinner while you move from group to group, repeating your invitation. Make a point of asking your guests to commence eating as soon as they are served, but don't press them, for many people prefer to wait for their host to begin.

Sensitive areas

For some people, good food, wine, and conversation are sufficient dinner entertainments. Others like to add music. If you do, take into consideration that lyrics or loud sound levels can distract guests, cut across conversations, and conflict with the party's mood of the moment. People's tastes are varied and some may not agree with your choice of music, but it will not be possible to please everyone.

Be sensitive, too, to attitudes to pets. Lots of people are frightened of dogs, allergic to cats, or just don't enjoy animals. If your pet fails to disappear by itself, remove it to a quiet, contained area, away from the guests.

And if other pet-loving guests start talking about theirs? Change the subject as deftly and as soon as you can unless the entire party seems to genuinely enjoy the conversation. Do the same whenever a guest seems stuck in a boring conversational groove and other guests look as though they need rescuing.

Once upon a time it was considered "bad form" socially to discuss servants, ill health, religion, politics, and sex. Scarcely anyone has servants anymore, but people do tend to talk on about their hairdressers and mechanics, their plumbers and drycleaners. And if there's anything more tedious than people talking about their ailments, it's fitness fanatics talking about their diets and their gym instructor. Religion and politics can still be problematic. And sex. But if no one seems disturbed by the conversation, let it flow.

Most adults tread cautiously with strangers on possibly controversial topics. If hostilities do break out or if someone's unpleasantly drunk, you might try taking aside anyone involved and then, as host, attempt to take control. You could say, perhaps, that they are making you unhappy and ask them to stop. If that has no effect, as nicely as you can, suggest that they might feel happier at home and offer to call a taxi cab. If you must ask a guest to leave, well, resist talking about them when they're gone. At such times, you might need to prevail upon the goodwill of other guests to assist you with the troublesome one. Make sure you thank them within a day or two of the incident.

These days, when people have such strong feelings about smoking, it's wise to let your guests know where you stand. Are your invitations conditional upon people not smoking? If you're blessed with a garden or balcony, you could designate that as a smokers' zone to be used before and after dinner. If you accept smoking, warn your non-smoking guests.

The meal

The dinner party itself usually consists of three courses: a first course, a main course, and finally pudding or dessert. The classic English nine-course dinner party is a rarity these days. It begins with soup or some other first course; second, fish; third, sorbet; fourth or main course of meat or game with vegetables, or salad (which may be served separately as a fifth course); sixth, pudding or dessert; seventh, "savoury"; eighth, cheese; and ninth, fruit.

The "savoury" is the rather quaint inclusion of a small course of something piquant, even salty or spicy, but not sweet. These days, it is more usually offered at the beginning of the meal as an hors d'oeuvres, which translates from French as "outside the main works" and once referred to what we now call side dishes. A savoury presented after the main course and salad indicates the end of the meal, that there is no dessert, cheese or fruit to follow.

For advice on setting the table, see page 24.

Servings should not be scanty, but neither should you risk overwhelming or embarrassing your guests by serving them huge portions that defeat their appetites. Do offer them second helpings as you progress through the meal, but don't insist if they decline.

With a larger dinner party, not buffet style, a host and a guest, or two hosts, can adapt the traditional serving practise by starting with the person on the host's right, then moving around the table to the left, serving their own plates as they continue in that direction. The table should be cleared from the left to the right. Food should be served from each person's right side and removed from their left.

Another option for the main course is for a host to move clockwise around the table, serving meat to each guest. Or you can serve each plate with meat and pass it along, with the guests serving themselves with vegetables. If you prefer, you can ask all your guests to serve themselves and others nearby with both meat and vegetables. The process will run smoothly if everyone passes the platters in one direction.

After the main course, avoid the messy (and noisy) business of stacking. Better that the hosts remove any unwanted plates two by two, and any tableware no longer needed.

Wine, including port served with the cheese and fruit, is poured with the right hand, and passed toward the left. A host might opt to walk clockwise around the table pouring each guest's first glass of wine, before placing the bottle on the table and asking people to help themselves to more. If there is more than a single host, one may choose to serve the wine (starting at the opposite end of the table and also moving clockwise) while the other serves the food. In this way, all guests will have both food and wine before them at about the same time.

For more advice on serving—and eating—different foods, see page 16.

Coffee and liqueurs at the table, or will you lead your guests back to the sitting room? Please yourself, or ask guests their preference. If you serve coffee at the table, it's more pleasant if any remaining dishes are first cleared.

Few women now choose to lead their female guests away from the table, leaving men to enjoy port and cigars. However, this point in the evening can be a good time to suggest guests swap seats and form new groupings, if you think it suitable.

Farewelling guests

When departure time approaches and your guests announce that they must leave, don't press them to linger. See them to your door, help them on with their coats, tell them how much you've enjoyed the pleasure of their company, and wish them farewell.

But what do you do when guests are having a great time but you're weary and wish they would leave? Stop serving drinks, ingenuously offer them "one last cup of coffee", and hope they'll take your hint without feeling their bonhomie is being rejected. Or perhaps you have a better way? Something sure to set your guests leaving but laughing. Something that epitomizes the spirit of etiquette in action—and will never be found in a rule book.

Hints for serving and eating

Certain foods commonly create either anxiety or curiosity among hosts and guests alike. Here are tips on serving and eating, including how to carve successfully, how to eat slithery spaghetti, and what foods you can politely tackle with your fingers.

Artichokes. Use your hands to pluck each of the outer leaves, and dip it in its dressing. Then suck the white fleshy base of each leaf, before discarding the remains to one side of your plate. When you reach the choke (the fibrous, thistly part), remove it, using a knife and fork to reveal and eat the artichoke's heart.

Asparagus. Canny cooks snap off the wooden base or peel the lower part of the stalk. Don't restrict the tactile pleasure of asparagus to your mouth alone. Use your fingers to hold them by their stalks and nibble from the tip down to where it may get stringy. But if you'd rather not, then use your knife and fork. A thoughtful host will provide fingerbowls or fingertowels as an optional item.

Avocados. Seek avocados that are "just right"; avoid ones that are rock hard or so ripe that the fruit subsides into a squishy mess at the slightest pressure of hand or knife. Gently but firmly holding the avocado, halve the fruit lengthwise with a very sharp, pointed knife. Then use both hands to jiggle and twist the halves apart. Remove the large stone from one half by pressing a sharp knife blade into the seed, twisting gently, and lifting out. You can then add dressing or pile each avocado cup with filling to eat with a small spoon from a small- to medium-sized plate or bowl (there are even dishes available that are specially designed to cradle avocado halves). Or you may peel, slice, and fan the fruit for serving. To do this, turn each half cut side down, divide into smaller segments if you think these would be more manageable, and peel. Use a pan slice to transfer a segment to a small, flat serving plate. With the point of a knife, cut fruit lengthwise into about four to five slices but leave them joined at one end. Take a rounded-end knife to gently ease apart the sliced end to form a fan of overlapping slices. Wipe away any smudges before adding accompaniments.

Bread and Bread Rolls. Before eating a slice of bread, cut it in half, then cut one of those halves into quarters. Each quarter is buttered in turn as one eats. Then do the same to the remaining half. Bread rolls are not cut with a knife but torn into bite-size pieces with the fingers, each being separated from the roll and buttered just before being eaten. For information on bread and butter plates and knives, see the section on table setting on page 24.

Butter. Gourmands prefer unsalted butter, but whether salted or not, it should never be so hard that a chainsaw is necessary to cut it, nor so soft that it's liquid. Present it on small platters, the butter either curled or sliced into manageable portions, a small knife or spatula with it. Each guest can then transfer to the side of their bread and butter plates a sufficient quantity to butter an entire serving of bread. If you set individual butter pots, guests can use their own butter knives for serving.

Cakes. Cake calls for cake or bread and butter plates, small cake forks and spoons, or small dinner forks and dessert spoons. Some cakes are manageable with a fork alone, held in the right hand. Use the side of the fork to break away pieces of cake, and then either the tines (prongs) or the bowl of the fork to carry each piece from plate to mouth. Very small, virtually bite-size cakes or petits fours (meaning "little ones from the oven") can be eaten with the fingers. If serving these, you could also serve fingertowels.

Canapés, Crudités, and Hors d'oeuvres. Fingers are both a simple and perfect tool but some nibbles will be best served and eaten with the aid of toothpicks. Either way, small napkins are a must for comfort, not only to wipe fingers but also to wrap used toothpicks when replacing them on the serving platter.

Caviar. Pile crushed caviar into a bowl with a serving scoop and surround with ice. Place a dollop of sour cream on toast, top with caviar and a squeeze of lemon. Very finely chopped boiled egg white and yolk (served separately) and finely chopped onion are also often served as condiments in separate bowls around the caviar.

Cheese. Serve selections of cheese on glass or ceramic platters or on wooden boards, with one or more knives depending on the size of the platter and the number of cheeses. Cheese knives are those with a curved tine or prong at the blade's end. But any sharp (not serrated), pointed knife will do. Guests cut their choice of one or two cheeses with the blade, using the end tip to deliver it to their plates, either their small side plates which they move to the middle of their place setting, or fresh plates served by their host.

Cheese is served with its rind on, with plain crackers at more formal meals, but with bread as well at less formal ones. It's served immediately after the main course, and with or without fruit unless the dessert course to follow is simply fresh fruit. Many accomplished home entertainers simply place cheese, fruit, and dessert on the table simultaneously so that their guests may sample all or none according to their tastes or dietary dictates.

Three to five cheeses provide a good mix. Cater to individual preferences and offer variety by choosing from cheeses with a strong or delicate taste, a firm or soft texture. If you're having a wine and cheese party, select as many cheeses as your heart desires or your budget can stand.

Chicken. Considerate hosts serving chicken legs, chicken wings, or marinated half-chickens, flattened but not boned, should also provide standby finger-bowls or fingertowels and receptacles for the bones. However, boned chicken fillets from any part of the bird are very easy to handle with knife and fork. See page 22 for information on how to carve a whole chicken.

Coffee. Coffee should be served with milk and/or cream, cubed or granular sugar, and/or coffee crystals. It may be offered demitasse (black, in tiny cups) or with milk or cream in a larger cup. It may be poured direct from a filter pot or made in a percolator, plunger, or in an espresso machine and transferred to a warmed coffee pot. It may be served directly at the table or in the surroundings of your choice with a tray, cups, saucers, spoons, and accompaniments set ready nearby. Some people prefer decaffeinated coffee, so it is a good idea to keep a small supply on hand.

Condiments. Serve chutneys, jams, mustards, pickles, and the like in individual small, shallow bowls on service dishes holding serving spoons or spatulas. Salt and pepper can also be served in this manner or in grinders—taste food before seasoning.

There is no need to provide a whole cluster of condiments for each individual, nor should you rely on just one pot of each to serve a large table. If only a reasonable number of condiments are being served, one pot of each between two is a luxury, and one between three or four quite adequate. If the meal is very informal, the serving ratio could stretch to one to eight. As the host, it is a friendly gesture first to offer to serve those seated either side of you, but there is no need to feel obliged since many people prefer to serve themselves. If there are several offerings, they might be gathered on a small tray or trays and handed around the table in one direction, following the host's serving of the food (see the etiquette section on page 10). Each person serves themselves to the side of their plate, preferably near the food the condiment will enhance.

Corn. Handling this vegetable has become so much easier with the invention of corn-on-the-cob servers: small handles with one or two prongs that can be implanted at each end of a cob. Spread butter and seasonings on one side before eating. As yet no arbiter of manners has dared to declare that a person should start eating from the left or right—just start at either end and work toward the other. If you start in the middle you are likely to end with your face smeared with butter. Even so, it could be a messy business so fingerbowls or fingertowels should be provided. There does seem to be a very practical move to slice corn into rounds from 1/2–1 inch (1–2 cm) in thickness before cooking. It is then easy to use a fork to pick up each slice through its middle, and nibble around the edges. For eating corn off the cob, see the section on peas on page 19.

Cutlery. When each course is finished, cutlery is placed side by side in the middle or slightly to the right of middle of the plate or bowl, handles resting over the edge nearest the diner. Bowls of forks and spoons face upward, knife blades toward the middle where they are less likely to cause harm. If you wish to rest your cutlery during a meal, lay it in a v-shape with the handles apart and resting over the sides of the plate, the other ends nearly touching, blades toward the middle, forks and spoons face downward.

Fingerbowls. There should be one fingerbowl for each guest and each bowl should be wide enough to hold a pair of hands, and deep enough to carry 2–3 inches (6–8 cm) of warm water without overflowing when fingertips are being rinsed. A slice of lemon or a squeeze of lemon juice may be added to the water to help clean greasy fingers. The bowl may be set on a small service dish immediately above each guest's place.

Fingertowels. These are small, moist towels, either sealed in foil or in a casserole dish and warmed in the oven, or left uncovered and chilled in the refrigerator. They are brought to the table on a tray, with serving tongs, to accompany the course for which they will be required, and either

handed round by the host or placed on the table for guests to help themselves. Individual small plates should be set immediately above each setting where the towels can rest during the course (towels can also be served on these plates). Another tray should be provided for the used fingertowels and removed before the next course is served. Some hosts choose to walk around distributing the towels only at the end of the course, but this is not quite as useful.

Finger Food and Messy Food. Finger food is not necessarily messy, nor messy food necessarily eaten with the fingers, but very often they are one and the same. Hosts and guests alike will be wise to graciously acknowledge the defeat of knife, fork, or spoon and use their hands when this is simplest; for instance, with canapés, crudités or hors d'oeuvres, crab, prawns, lobster, fruit, and sandwiches.

But avoid little fingers crooked to dislocation in misguided attempts at gentility or daintiness.

With famously messy foods such as corn-on-the-cob, pasta, and lobster, hosts should provide fingerbowls, fingertowels, and plenty of small or large napkins as appropriate. With finger food and messy food, you should also supply dishes to collect the debris, such as toothpicks, wrappings, and bones.

If you have a collection of bibs and tuckers, offer them to your guests. Men once used bibs tied round their neck and women lace or muslin squares (tuckers) tucked over their bodice necklines. At some stage, the bib became known as a bib and tucker when it became more triangular in shape, slotted in one corner so an opposite, narrowed corner could be tucked. Hosts may improvize with very large napkins tucked in at the neck but might need to lead the way so that their guests feel comfortable about adopting this tactic. Many people feel uncomfortable in this regalia, so this must remain a matter of choice.

Fish. Specially designed fish knives and forks are smaller than main course cutlery. Usually wider than most dinner knives, the blunt blade of a fish knife rounds to a curved tip on the upper edge. It is used like a spatula so does not need to be held as a dinner knife. The method for cutting up a fish is similiar, whether you as host are serving individual portions from a whole fish, or whether as a guest you are presented with a smaller whole fish. For details, see the section on carving on page 23.

Fruit. Berries can be served in a large central bowl, not too deep or they'll squash each other. They can then be served into separate bowls and accompaniments can be added from separate servers for cream (thin or thick), icing (powdered) sugar, and orange zest.

Fruit compote is best served in individual dishes. This way the server can make sure everyone gets a bit of everything. When people serve themselves from one large central bowl, not only is it difficult for them not to spill the juices or pieces of fruit, but one guest may end up with all the plums, another with all the grapes.

Citrus fruit, such as oranges and grapefruit, are best cleaned of peel, pith, and the fine inner skin-like membrane. Then slice them into thin rounds (not so thin that they fall apart) and remove all pips. Finely dust each slice with icing (powdered) sugar or splash with a liqueur marinade if desired, and arrange on a central platter or individual plates. For cutlery, use special, small knives and forks for eating fruit, or a small dessert or dinner fork and knife.

Mangoes deserve special mention. Cut them into halves lengthwise with a sharp knife—the halves will be uneven, as you must slice to avoid the stone. Repeat to free the flesh from the side with the stone. Now peel and slice in the same manner used for avocadoes (see page 16), or use the knife to cut a crisscross pattern of shapes approximately 1/2 inch (1 cm) square, cutting down to, but not through, the skin. Pick up each mango half and with your fingertips put slight pressure on the skin from below as though to turn the half inside out. The little squares of mango flesh pop up for easy eating or scooping out to serve.

Other fruit with a core, stone, or pips (such as apples, apricots, melons, nectarines, papayas, peaches, pears, pineapples, and plums) should be peeled and all these inner bits removed. To prepare stone fruit, slice them in half around the stone and then gently twist both halves in opposite directions to separate them. Use the tip of a knife or a grapefruit spoon (with a serrated edge) to help remove stones that won't come away easily. Then slice into either rounds or wedges, or use a melon baller if you want to be a little fancy. Baste with a pastry brush dipped in fresh lime or lemon juice to help stop the fruit turning brown.

Cherries and grapes, however, do not require deseeding. They can be eaten with the fingers, although grape scissors are a nice touch with a communal bowl of grapes. To dispose of the pips, lightly cup one hand, move it close to your mouth, and gently drop the pips into it, before putting them to one side of your plate.

If whole fruits are served to guests, the individual will have to cut the fruit for themselves on separate small to medium plates set for the purpose after the previous course has been cleared, or on their bread and butter or side plates. Apples and pears are halved, then one half is quartered, with each quarter cored and peeled as it's eaten, either with the fingers or by using knife and fork to cut crosswise into bite and fork-size pieces. The second half is given the same treatment. Oranges and other citrus fruit are first peeled, then halved, one half quartered, each quarter pipped and eaten as for apples and pears. With stone fruit such as apricots, remove the stone as described previously. Then quarter and eat using fingers or fork. If the stone fruit is small, eat whole, and remove the stone as though it were a cherry pip.

Nuts. Small, shelled nuts that are served with drinks before dinner are eaten with the fingers. Resist the temptation to scoop up an entire handful as they will prove difficult to manage. Bowls of large, unshelled nuts (such as brazil nuts) and a nutcracker may accompany the cheese and fruit course at table. When eating, select one or two nuts and use the nutcracker on your own plate to shell them, before returning the instrument to the bowl. If you have difficulty cracking a nut, you could ask a companion to help, or leave the nut on the side of your plate.

Pasta. Eating ribbon pasta such as fettuccine, linguine, spaghetti, and tagliatelle is quite an art. You only have to watch a child grappling with the noodles, a face covered in sauce, to recall how difficult it can be. In 19th-century Naples, people ate it with their hands!

Such pasta is best dealt with by first using your fork to separate a few strands. Then with the tines (prongs) gently pressed to the plate's surface, pivot the fork to wind the pasta strands slowly but firmly around the tines. If you can manage with fork alone, the custom is to use the right hand. If you need your spoon as well, then the left hand takes the fork, the right the spoon. If you try to take too much at once, it will slither away from you, often while your fork is halfway to your mouth. If this does happen, let it go and start again. On no account make an open-mouthed lunge for it. Nor should you cut the pasta into small pieces.

Pâté and Terrine. Either the smooth paste that is pâté or a more roughly textured terrine may be presented for a first course as individual servings, each with their own selection of crackers or toast and a small spreader knife. Or either dish might be passed around with pre-dinner drinks from a lipped tray (to prevent slippery accidents and help people to help themselves) plus knife.

Peas. These little green balls can be a real problem. Use your dinner knife to push (in truth, squash) a few peas at a time onto the end of your fork. If you are happy to mix the foods on your plate as you eat, other foods can be helpful carriers for peas. Or you can put down your knife, and with your right hand use your fork as a spoon.

Potatoes. However they're cooked (baked, steamed, or fried) or however presented (in their jackets, sliced in rounds or wedges), simply cut to bite size with knife and fork and then use the fork in either left or right hand to carry the vegetable to your mouth. If you're presented with a potato wrapped in foil, use your knife and fork preferably—but fingers if necessary—to remove the foil before cutting. Mashed potatoes may be eaten by using the fork in the right hand as a spoon. It is not polite to eat french fries and the like with your fingers unless served in a very casual manner or unless fingerbowls or towels are supplied.

Salad. Thoughtful hosts do not serve monstrous salads in huge bowls with enormous servers. They provide maneuverable servers with salads broken into very manageable pieces, lightly coated with dressing, never swimming in it. Even better: they present their guests with individual pre-served salads that can be eaten with fork alone, but also supply each guest with a knife in case they need extra assistance. It is the American custom to serve salad before the main course. Elsewhere, if separate salad plates are to be used, the hosts first remove the dinner plates and then set smaller, medium-sized plates for the salad. Or these may be set above the side or bread and butter plates. If separate plates are not provided, then guests use their dinner plates or, if these are loaded with debris, the side or bread and butter plates can be brought to the middle of their place settings to take salad.

Sauces. It's a good idea to serve sauce in a sauceboat or a bowl, each with its own service dish and spoon, to avoid the awkwardness and mess that often accompanies the attempt to extract sauce from a bottle. Each guest can then pour or spoon sauce near or over their food according to taste.

Shellfish. Clams, mussels, and oysters are eaten with a special small fork or with a small dinner fork set to the far right of the setting for use in the right hand. The left hand is used to steady the shell or plate. With the flesh secure on the fork, dip it into any accompanying sauce, perhaps having first peppered and juiced the whole platter to taste with the traditional lemon wedge.

Prawns and shrimp can be eaten with the fingers. First remove the head, then the tail and body shell. Very tiny shrimp with thin shells virtually indistinguishable from their flesh are simply spooned up.

Crabs and lobsters need to have their tough shells split or cracked so that the rich meat can be extracted. If lobster is served to you whole, use one hand to hold the main body on the plate, the other to twist off the appendages if shears are not provided. Still holding the lobster, break off the tail, and using shears or a knife, cut each side of the thin underside. Then remove the tail meat with your fork for cutting into smaller pieces. Suck the meat from the ends of the small claws. Fingers can be used to break into the larger ones at the second joint and along the side—shears or nutcrackers will help. Lobsters and crabs are often sliced lengthwise down the back from head to tail to help diners. Once the meat is available, use fingers, fork, or spoon to eat. The tamale (the green liver) and the roe (the female's tiny red eggs) are considered delicacies. Fingerbowls and towels are a must, some would say bibs and tuckers too.

Skewered Food. Hold the skewer in one hand with the point lightly but firmly held to the surface of your plate at an angle of 45° or less. Use a fork in your other hand to ease food piece by piece from the skewer, moving it to the side. If some pieces stick, place the skewer on your plate and use a knife and fork to trim the food from the sides. Remove all the food from one skewer before eating and moving on to the next. Place empty skewers to one side of your plate.

Soup. A soup spoon has a shallow bowl and a near circular rim. Customarily, you should scoop the soup away from yourself, toward the far side of the bowl, and then sip from the side of the spoon if liquid only, or from the front or tip of the spoon if it contains solid morsels. This is no longer a golden rule, although it is easier to avoid spilling soup into your lap if you are using your free hand to tip your bowl away from you rather than toward you. But then, it's polite to leave a little rather than risk clanging around the base of your soup bowl in any direction. If the bowl comes with a service dish, leave your spoon on the dish when you've finished. Otherwise, leave it in the bowl. In either case, leave the bowl of the spoon facing upward.

Wrapping Papers and Other Debris. It truly is amazing the amount of paper and other debris that can accumulate with a meal. Thoughtful hosts will provide a small receptacle at the left of the setting for such remnants. If there is no receptacle for that purpose, guests simply leave such items on their plates but to one side. If a real nuisance, they may remove them to their side plates but, if at all possible, should avoid placing them directly on the table.

How to carve

"Have you learned to carve well?" Lord Chesterfield wrote to his son in 1748. "For it is ridiculous not to carve well ... do you use yourself to carve adroitly and genteely, without hacking half an hour across a bone, without bespattering the company with the sauce, and without overturning the glasses into your neighbour's pocket?"

A skilled carver, then as now, is much admired. It is an old tradition for hosts to compliment their guests, male or female, by requesting that they carve. And the old techniques still apply, although these days we are not so concerned with the "correctness" of the cut.

There are a few essentials for good carving. It begins with only a little practise, and you need a sharp carving knife, either stainless or carbon steel, plus a two-pronged carving fork with a fingerguard—both should be good and strong with comfortable handles. A friendly butcher will show you how to sharpen your carving knife, perhaps even do it for you, or you may take it to your local knife sharpener periodically to maintain its edge in top condition.

Experience and personal choice will bring many variations, although there are usually four basic knives in the carver's armory:

~ the boner, with a flexible blade about 5 inches (12 cm) long, used to produce thin slices near bones or in other difficult to reach places, and especially in fine-textured flesh such as ham;

~ a slicer, with a 9–14-inch (22–35-cm) blade about 1 inch (2.5 cm) wide, to access smaller cuts of meat, especially poultry and game;

~ one carver, with a wide, firm blade, at least 7 inches (17 cm) long, often longer, to cut through gristle and bone and useful with larger cuts of meat, especially those on the bone;

~ and a chef's knife, with an even heavier, triangular blade, about 8 inches (20 cm) long, for flat carving of large sections of meat.

It's fine to choose from an electric carving knife's assorted blades, although this is better used out of guest's earshot in the kitchen. The knack here is to let the knife do the work. You simply guide the blades and exert a light pressure to slice across the grain.

Whatever the knife, or whether carving at table, on the sideboard, or in the kitchen, the traditional carving board with a trench to catch juices provides a sure surface. Have a warmed platter plus cover standing by so that the flesh does not go cold between carving and serving.

Beef

To carve a sirloin (the upper part of the loin) roast, place the side with the most meat uppermost and so that the t-bone stem points toward you. Cut straight to the bone at a thumb's length from the larger end, using the knife point to slice along the bone to remove the formed wedge of beef. Then use the knife point to remove fat and gristle from the chine (the curved, bony plate formed by back and loin bones). Carve at an angle of about 30° to the bone.

Another way to carve a sirloin roast is to carve thin slices down and inward toward you along the t-bone stem. Then, slide the knife under the meat and along the upper surface of the stem. Do the same along the upper arm of the t-bone to release the slices. Turn the joint over, and if it will hold steady, repeat as for the first side. Otherwise, remove the meat from the bone before slicing the second side.

To carve a fillet of beef, temporarily compress its already fine texture by holding it firm with the back of the fork tines while using a long slicing knife. Starting from the wider end of the meat, carve slices about ½ inch (1 cm) thick, keeping the blade straight but drawing toward you as you cut downward.

A rolled rib or rolled sirloin roast can be placed either on its side or on end for carving. When carving on end, insert the carving fork on one side about 1 inch (2.5 cm) below the top before slicing across the grain, making the first slice thick if necessary to make a level carving guide. Keep moving the fork down as you carve, removing the string trussing as the knife meets them. When down to the last couple of inches, cut the meat in half across the top. Place each

HOW TO CARVE A SIRLOIN ROAST

1. Place the side with the most meat uppermost on a cutting board or platter. Starting at the larger end of the roast, cut a piece from the end. With the point of the knife, cut under the piece to remove it from the bone.

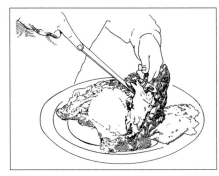

2. With the point of the knife, remove the fat and gristle from the chine (the curved bony plate).

3. Carve in thin slices from the fat side at an angle of 30° to the bone. Hold the carving knife with your thumb against the handle and your forefinger pressed against the back of the blade. This grip gives the greatest control.

portion with its cut surface down and complete the slicing.

A standing (or bone-in) rib roast is best placed with its broadest side down, the rib tips (the narrower end) pointing to the right. To carve individual slices, insert the fork through the side to hold the roast firmly in place, slice horizontally across the grain to the ribs and withdraw the knife. Repeat to the bottom of the first rib. Use the knife tip to cut close along the rib.

To carve an entire rib, cut between the first and second ribs working from the rib tips inward to the broader end.

Chicken

One way to carve a chicken is to first sever the thigh and drumstick as one from the body then separate them at the second joint. Cut the wings from the body at the second joint. Slice horizontally along the bottom of the breast. Next cut slices down the breast, starting from the outside and working in. Repeat for the other side.

A second method involves leaving the wings in place but removing the legs. Separate thigh and drumstick. Then carve slices from the outside until close to the breastbone. As you go, press the slices to the outside. Detach the carved flesh by slicing over the ribs, removing one wing and one half-breast in a piece from the carcass. Repeat on the remaining side. The wings may be separated from the half-breast portions before serving.

Turkey

This can be carved in the same manner as a chicken. In addition, you may want to slice dark meat from the drumstick: hold the narrow end and carve downward. If the breast section becomes too wide for easy slicing, continue to carve at the same angle but from front and back ends in turn so slices are manageable. Spoon stuffing onto the serving platter with the sliced turkey before carving the second side.

Duck

Although a duck can also be carved in the same manner as a chicken, you can obtain more flesh by pulling meat from the bone rather than carving it in the strict sense of the word. Start with the legs pointing to your right, sever the skin where the nearside leg joins the carcass. Turn the bird on its side, hold firmly with one fork in the cavity and with another, pull this leg from the body, cutting the connecting tissue at the joint. Cut the severed leg in two at the second joint. To halve the breast, slice downward from neck to tail, through the bone at each end. Remove one half-breast and wing by pulling with one fork while holding the carcass cavity firm with another fork. Pull the ribs from the severed half-breast before quartering or slicing.

Ham

Set the ham down on its flattest (inner) side. Near the shank (the narrower end), use your carving knife to cut straight to the leg bone. Move 2 inches (5 cm) up the slope of the leg and make another cut at a slant to connect with the first. Remove this wedge, which should be very fatty. With your knife at an angle of about 30° to the bone, carve

HOW TO CARVE POULTRY

 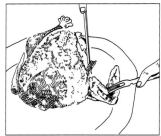 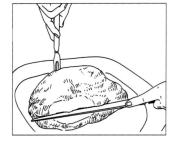 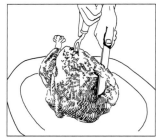

1. Place the bird, breast up, on a cutting board or platter. Cut through the skin between the leg and body, and push leg to the side with the knife to expose the joint. Slice through the cartilage between the bones to remove the leg.

2. Push down the wingtip with the fork to expose the joint and cut through with the tip of the knife to remove the wing.

3. Make a horizontal slice near the bottom of the breast so that meat will come off easily when carved.

4. Remove the breast meat from the bone from each side of the bird by carving down and on an angle in thin slices, starting from the outside and working in until close to the breastbone.

about one third of the ham into thin, even slices. Or, make a series of vertical cuts to the bone along the rounded side, working from upper to lower leg, pushing each slice toward the shank before inserting the knife at one end to run back along the bone to free the slices. When the first side is sliced, the ham is turned over.

Fish

As a guest presented with most small to medium whole fish, you may find it easier to place the fish so that it is at an angle of 45°, with the head pointing away to the left, the tail to the right, the spine to the left and the belly to the right. Use your fish knife (but any knife is acceptable) and fork to cut off the head and tail and place them to the side of your plate or to a separate bowl or plate if provided. If severing is difficult, either use a sharper dinner knife if one is at hand or leave the fish intact.

To remove the skin, run your knife down the fish's spine to split the skin, then take one end and lift and roll it toward you before setting it aside. You may prefer to eat the flesh from this skinless side, then remove the backbone and flip the fish over to skin and eat the second side. Or you may choose to skin both sides first.

To remove a portion of fish, work from where the head joins the body. Make a cut the length of one portion along the middle of the upper side. Next, cut around the head, then make a third cut equal to the first along the near edge of the fish. Then complete the portion with a cut across the top of the fish. Cut and eat the fish portion by portion.

To remove the backbone, work from the tail end and use the hooked tip of the fish knife to lever the backbone up and away. Or hold the tail end of the spine, slide under the knife, and gently ease the spine away from the flesh working toward the head.

If you are a host serving from one large fish, the principles are basically the same, although the portions will be larger. It is preferable to work with a fish knife, and you may find a flat server useful to slide under each serving portion while using another flat server to steady and protect the portion from collapse as you transfer it to a guest's plate. Cut and serve the fish portion by portion.

With trout, a guest requires a different technique. Remove the head, tail, and all skin then hold down the fish with the back of your fork while pressing the outside of the flesh with the flat of your knife, so that the narrow strip of fine bones is pushed out of the belly slit. Slit further and spread open the fish into its lengthwise halves, then remove the backbone.

With sole, after removing the skin, cut off the fine bony fringe at the sides of the belly. Then separate the upper fillets from the backbone by holding the fish in place with your fork and gently using your knife to push them to either side. You may now eat these upper fillets or proceed to free the lower fillets. Tease the lower fillets away from the backbone, working from the head to tail, then remove the backbone using one of the methods described above.

HOW TO SERVE A WHOLE FISH

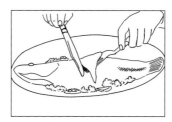 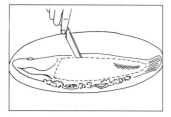  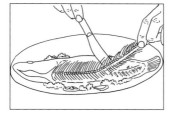

1. You may wish to remove the head and tail first. If removing skin, run the knife down the spine to split the skin, then lift and roll towards you.

2. With a fish knife, make a cut down the spine of the fish, and then cut around the head and down the side of the fish (the size of this portion will vary according to the situation).

3. Cut the fish into a portion sized for serving or eating. Slide the knife under this section and lift it away from the bone. Keep it steady with a fork.

4. After the top two sides are cut away, remove the spine (and head and tail if still attached) by lifting from the tail end and sliding the knife underneath.

The table

No matter how casual or formal the occasion, a table set with care and flair to receive guests is a sight that triggers a sense of excited anticipation; one born of memories of past conviviality, good food and wine, and above all, good friends and companions.

A table setting should be coordinated, but that doesn't mean everything must match; your home doesn't have to be equipped to equal the grand dining room of a five-star hotel. On the contrary, you can try mixing things, play at creating fresh combinations and effects. To this end, why not borrow occasionally from your family or close friends if they have items that will suit your table-setting purposes better than your own.

The tablecloth

For a formal table, first comes the cloth or place mats, or both. Extra mats can be used to hold hot platters. A white tablecloth is always a symbol to me of a special occasion, although as you can see from the Christmas chapter, a rich, polished wooden top is equally formal and superbly anchors the look and mood of the setting. Cloths should be large enough to hang halfway from tabletop to floor. As a general rule, it is best to avoid longer cloths as guests may get their feet caught up in the folds. Or you could fix a longer cloth back at each table leg to avoid tripping your guests. The tabletop-to-floor look is very elegant, however, as you can see in the photographs in the chapters "A Buffet" and "A Wedding at Home".

The place settings

There are so many ways in which to set a table; only you can decide what will work best in your home, taking into account your menu and number of courses, how formal the occasion is, your store of china, cutlery and glasses, the number of guests, and the size of your dining table.

Wherever you settle on the formality scale, it is pleasant for guests to have a selection of fresh plates. Then they don't need to be excessively dainty to avoid plunging their salad into a puddle of sauce if a separate plate is not provided.

Service plates, large plates about 10 inches (27 cm) across, are set at each place as bases for each plate used by a guest throughout the meal.

Both American and European styles set a small bread and butter plate to the left of the forks. Unless another, medium-sized plate is brought to the table, the European way is to use the bread and butter plate and knife for cheese, particularly at less formal occasions. Diners move these to the middle of their settings when the cheese, traditionally served on a wooden board, is brought to the table. As part of the American style setting, a medium-sized salad plate is placed at the upper left, above and almost touching the bread and butter plate.

If the menu includes foods that will generate bones, leaves, seeds, or other remnants of feasting, cater for these with a small dish set to the far left, beside the bread and butter plate, and leave space above the middle of each setting for a fingerbowl or a plate to hold a fingerbowl or two.

from left to right: *cheese knife, butter knife, snail (escargot) fork, oyster, grapefruit spoon, parfait spoon, teaspoon, soup spoon, medium spoon (used for desserts or pasta), tablespoon, fish fork, fish knife, steak knife, small knife (used for first courses, cheese, or fruit, or as a butter knife), small fork (used for first courses, pasta, salad, dessert, or fruit), large knife, large fork.*

Some scaling-down of the formality may suit smaller occasions or, for that matter, smaller tables. Remember, too, a platoon of tableware can create a cluttered tablescape, and one where the settings transform guests into islands unto themselves, their prospects for conviviality remote. So, whatever the menu, it is a good idea not to set more than three forks to the left of each plate and three knives plus the oyster fork to the right. If more cutlery is necessary, set it before serving that course.

The European way is to set forks to the diner's left, knives and spoons to the right, in the order in which they'll be used, working from the outside to the inside (nearest the plate). If there's a course requiring only a small fork (perhaps oysters, or cake), this fork is placed to the right, in course order. Knife blades are turned toward the plate, forks with their prongs upward and spoons resting on their backs. In many European countries, however, it is not unusual to find forks and spoons set face down and knives with their tips held by knife rests indicating that this cutlery is to be used for more than one course.

The middle of each setting is about 2 feet (60 cm) from the next. If space is tight, you can set either the dessert spoon and fork, or the fruit knife and fork, and a coffee spoon with either, horizontally above the plate.

This variation forms the American style. The small fork is set nearest to the plate and pointing to the right, its knife or spoon above and pointing to the left. The coffee spoon also points to the left.

Napkins folded to stand upright are placed mid-setting between knives and forks. Flat-folded napkins are traditionally placed on bread and butter plates, although larger ones can also be placed between knife and fork. For more about napkin-folding, see page 28.

Topple-proof place cards are often used for formal or larger events. You can find useful advice about these in the chapter on etiquette (see page 10).

Don't forget salt and pepper shakers, grinders, or bowls. Nor butter and mustard in small bowls or pots with under-

dishes and servers. Place them so that they are easily shared between two to six places and you'll avoid lots of bother as they're passed from guest to guest.

For information on serving particular foods, see page 16.

Glasses

In both American and European settings, glasses are traditionally placed above the spoons and knives in the order of use, the first glass being set about 1 inch (2-3 cm) above the tip of either the innermost or main knife. The others march forth behind it at an angle of 45°, either from left to right, right to left, or to form a triangle. Many people prefer to arrange their glasses in terms of height, placing them so that no glass hides another.

Although a good, all-purpose wine glass will serve very well, specifically designed glasses do make a substantial difference to the taste of wine. You can prove it to yourself if you have the opportunity to taste the same wine from several differently shaped glasses. All the components defining the shape of a glass (its surface area, depth, the slope of its sides, its rim circumference) direct the way wine enters the mouth and the taste-buds register response. The tip of the tongue is particularly sensitive to sweet tastes, the mid-tongue to acidic ones, the back to bitterness, and the sides to saltiness.

Whether crystal (very fine glass that "sings" when lightly flicked with your fingernail) or something less fine, all glassware should be spotless and smearless. The recipe for sparkling glasses? Double-rinse in hot water with a couple of lemon skins and allow to drain dry, upside down with rims resting on a paper towel or kitchen towel. Finish with a lint-free polishing cloth.

from left to right: *small liqueur, sherry, port, white wine, red wine, champagne flute, champagne saucer, balloon, cocktail glass, beer glass.*

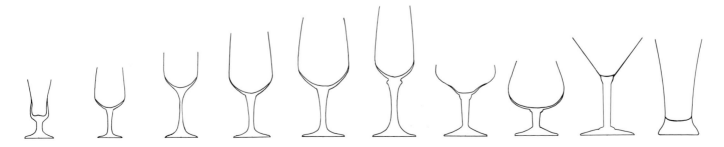

Lighting

Candlelight can turn a table into an oasis of light, glassware sparkling and silver gleaming as the flames burn. And it is flattering for people, too. There's no need to save candles for evening events. If your dining room is gloomy, or there's a dull, dark, or stormy day outside your windows, use candles to light up a lunch party or afternoon tea. Place them with care; candles are tedious if they block the sight-lines between guests seated on opposite sides of the table. Candle flames should be kept at least 2 inches (5 cm) below seated eye-level. Moreover, it can be quite disorientating for a seated guest to glance upward at very tall candles because, from that angle, any listing to one side is magnified. A good rule of thumb is: the taller the candlestick, the shorter the candle; the shorter the candle, the taller the

candlestick. And do make sure you have plenty of them unless you are trying to create a spooky effect. Even a romantic dinner for two requires reasonable light—if too dim, it can be more aggravating than seductive.

White candles are always attractive, but natural beeswax and dyed ones can be just what a table needs. Dripless candles are the answer to messy cleanups. Be careful with scented candles — a dining room that was subtly fragrant when the soup was served can be quite oppressive by the time dessert comes around. Rely on your food to contribute pleasant aromas to the occasion — and flowers (see the chapter on floral decoration, page 32).

Buffet tables present a different set of options, which are covered in a special chapter (see page 148).

The art of napkin folding

oven, or promise a welcome chill fresh from the refrigerator to sticky hands.

On our laps are our trusty napkins. And they will stay there, and not slip to the floor, if you fold them into a triangle with the longest side across your thighs from left to right, and the opposite point resting on your knees. It also helps if you don't wriggle around a lot and are not wearing slithery clothes.

It is a matter of taste as to whether quartered plain white linen napkins, or perhaps triangles or oblongs laid on the butter or dinner plates, appeal to you more than elaborate embroidery or remarkable folds.

Folded napkins are like Christmas crackers—items of momentary and ephemeral pleasure. When I was younger, I went through a stage when the more fancily folded the napkin, the more impressed I was. Now I choose folds that don't demand the skills of a dedicated origami practitioner. Nor do I want my guests to so admire my napkin artistry that they are daunted at the prospect of using them and thus destroying my handiwork. If an intricately folded napkin requires a rather violent shake in order to set it free, the chances are that a glass will be knocked over before the meal's even begun.

My choice of folds is usually influenced by the mood I plan to create with my table setting. But it might also depend on the mood I'm in; that is, whether I'm in keep-it-simple mode or feeling more frivolous. And then, my children like to do our napkins and so it's often their personal choice which graces our table.

A napkin cannot stand unsupported without starch in the fabric, so some folds will not be possible without well-starched napkins. This is simply done with spraystarch and

*T*able napkins—where would we be without them? In quite a mess, I think. Wiping greasy fingers on our clothes or, as our forebears did, on pieces of bread which they then tossed to their dogs.

Serving an equally useful purpose are the bibs with ties or tuck-in ends which are used when something delicious but splashy is served to tempt our palates, such as mussel soup or bouillabaisse. Then there are the hot or cold (depending on the climate) fingertowels that thoughtful hosts will have on hand if their menu requires them. They're usually white, soft, and have been carefully dampened so they are neither soggy nor barely moist. Some hosts like to add lemon juice to the dampener, or a scant touch of the lightest cologne. Lay them out in a row on a tray, where they will steam slightly after being wrapped in foil in the a steam iron, but there are also plenty of intriguing ways to fold napkins that will lie flat but attractively on your table.

It is easier to work with truly square napkins than circular or oblong ones, and the larger the napkin, the more splendid the effect and less difficult it is to achieve. To my mind, a good, all-purpose napkin is white and between 20 and 24 inches (50 and 60 cm) square.

The napkin must also be quite flat before you start folding. Any existing creases will interfere with the napkin's

capacity to hold folds and be self-supporting. An ironing tip: first iron the corners and sides of a napkin or tablecloth so it's square when you finish. And a word of warning to beginners: beware patterned napkins. Unless they're double-sided, it will try your patience attempting to fold them so that only the right side shows.

Finally, the best-kept napkin-folding secret of all: it's easier than it looks, or reads. Just take your time and go step by step.

The Candle

One of the easiest, and most elegant, napkin folds is the Candle.

(1) Fold a starched, square napkin in half, from one diagonally opposite point to another, to form a triangle.

(2) Turn up the folded edge about 1 inch (2.5 cm).

(3) Turn the napkin over and lie it flat on the table. The folded-edge face of the napkin triangle should be on the downside. The folded-edge itself should be the one nearest you.

(4) Take the lower left corner of the triangle and roll across to the right, leaving just as much as you need to tuck the lower right corner into the fold.

(5) As a finishing touch you can also tuck in a sprig of something from your garden, perhaps holly at Christmas to hint at Christmas candles. Further up the Candle's stem, you can tuck in a smallish place card if you wish.

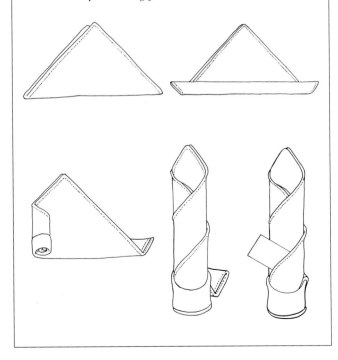

The Inverted Sail

This fold is also known as the Muldeva. It is a good, all-purpose fold, and very stable.

(1) Turn your square, flat, starched napkin to make a diamond in front of you.

(2) Take the top point to the bottom point to form a triangle.

(3) Take the top left and top right corners of this triangle to meet at its bottom point. You now have another diamond.

(4) Take the bottom point and fold the diamond's lower half under to form another triangle.

(5) Fold either the left or right half back.

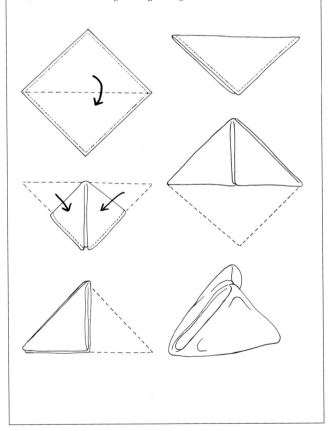

The Fan

Children love this fold. It is simple but to succeed it is absolutely essential to use large, heavyweight paper napkins or big linen ones.

(1) Start by folding the napkin in half and position it in front of you so that the free edges are to the left, the centerfold to the right.

(2) In the lower quarter, with the bottom edge pointing upward, form two pleats.

(3) Turn the napkin over so that the pleats are on the downside, the unpleated quarter on the upside. Turn it clockwise so that the two, free corner flaps are at the upper right.

(4) Then fold the bottom edge to meet the top edge.

(5) Take the top, right corner and fold the narrow, unpleated part of the napkin so that its top edge sits beside the pleats.

(6) Fold its flap under, alongside the fold in the pleat to its left.

(7) Stand the napkin with the pleats facing you and adjust the fan.

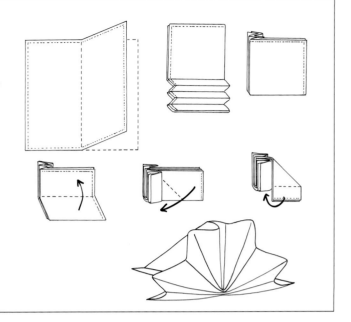

The Cone

Also known as the Boat, this fold appeals to children, many adults, and is beloved by novice folders.

(1) Fold a starched napkin from top to bottom to form a rectangle.

(2) Take the top right corner over and start rolling all the way over to the napkin's left edge.

(3) Then turn back the flap formed by the lower right corner so that you have an even base on which to stand your cone, plus two decorative flaps, one at the base and one at the side.

(4) To make the cone more stable, after you fold up the bottom flap, you can fold it once again to form a cuff. So with the cone, too, there's somewhere to slide a flower or card.

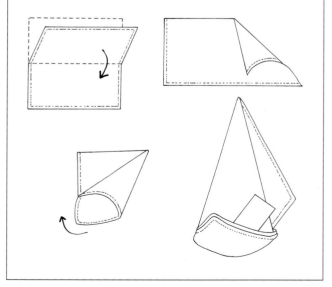

The Americana

This classic fold lets you use your collection of napkin rings.

(1) Fold a square napkin into quarters on the table and position to form a diamond with the four, free corners at the top.

(2) Fold the bottom and sides so that their points meet in the middle of the diamond. At this stage, you might want to insert a single-stemmed flower, perhaps a rose for a lover you're entertaining tête-à-tête.

(3) Turn in the right side, and then the left, so that the napkin is folded in thirds.

(4) Slip on a napkin ring or tie with a ribbon.

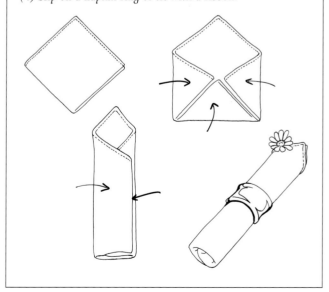

The Lily

Something pretty to blossom out of your table glasses.

(1) Fold a square napkin into quarters on the table and position to form a diamond with the four, free corners at the top.

(2) Fold the bottom folded point to the middle of the diamond.

(3) Then fold the right-hand point of the diamond over to meet the left-hand one.

(4) If you wish, you can now pleat each half. Otherwise, simply hold the fold at the base of the napkin and separate each flap or "petal" before placing in a glass.

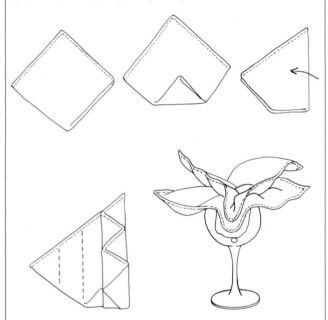

The Rose

This fold is the same as the Lily with one small variation and an extra, last step.

(1) Follow the instructions for the Lily up to, and including, step 3.

(2) Put the folded napkin into the glass before you separate the petals.

(3) After you've separated them, tuck each petal's tip into the middle.

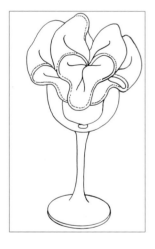

The Stripe

The Stripe is a fold you can do with unstarched fabric.

(1) Fold a square napkin in half to form a rectangle.

(2) Then fold it in half again to form a small square of four layers of fabric. Position this on the table to face you with the four, free corners at the upper right corner of the small square formed by the quartered napkin.

(3) Take the corner of the top layer back toward the central folding point, and fold the point over and under and out of sight.

(4) Take the corner of the second layer and slip it in behind the fold of the first.

(5) Take the corner of the third layer and slip it behind the fold of the second to form three even, diagonal "stripes".

(6) Fold the napkin into three by turning back the left and right sides in turn. Insert a place card, flower, or some other small treat.

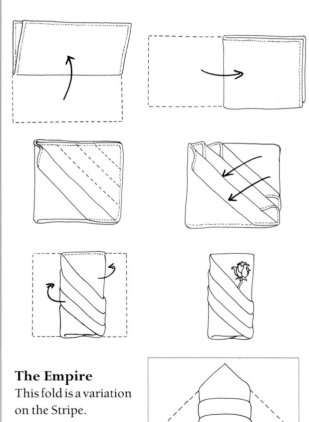

The Empire

This fold is a variation on the Stripe.

(1) Place the quartered napkin to form a diamond shape with the four, free corners at the top.

(2) Fold and tuck the three flaps as instructed for the Stripe, but, for the last fold, turn the upper left and lower right corner to the back.

Floral decoration

Whether you are having friends over for a lazy Sunday breakfast or a formal dinner party, the inclusion of flowers will always lift the spirit and give a festive feel to the occasion.

Unless that occasion is a grand one such as a wedding, the secret of success when arranging flowers at home is to make things simple and in keeping with the theme of the food itself. Don't overpower your guests with massive arrangements that they can't see over, and try to resist cluttering the table with so much tricky flora that there is no room left for serving plates. A lovely jug of daisies on the breakfast table cannot be beaten for freshness and simplicity.

Picnics and barbecues need not miss out on decoration, although using fine vases and delicate flowers would not be practical. Rather, try utilizing some of the ingredients of the meal to provide interest: bowls of fragrant herbs, bright red tomatoes or sunny lemons with the leaves still attached. Or some of the fresh plants in your surroundings: a few branches from a camellia perhaps, or a sprig of jasmine. You may be visiting a local area for your picnic. Why not keep an eye out for flowers along the way. Plants such as cosmos, clover, dandelions, wild grasses, nasturtiums, and buttercups can be found by the side of the road in many areas, and a bunch can provide a cheerful and effective decoration for a picnic.

Similarly, a simple supper or cosy winter lunch may not warrant elaborate flowers. A fantasy of exotics such as gourds or a bowl of baby vegetables will handsomely fit the setting and may even be munched by your guests along the way. But at afternoon teas with their old world charm, the setting really calls for roses, in particular the blousy old-fashioned garden varieties. Even if you don't grow roses yourself, try searching out a florist who supplies these beauties rather than the small-headed types grown in glass houses. Even if your roses are past perfection, you can still use the petals as table decorations, or frozen either in decorative ice blocks to float in a cool refreshment, or as part of an ice bowl in which the punch can be served (see the instructions for making an ice bowl on page 33).

More formal occasions such as cocktail or dinner parties will obviously require a more dramatic treatment. Let the room, the table and its accessories, the food, and the season dictate the decoration. Trailing arrangements can be used

Keeping flowers fresh

~ Once flowers have been out of water for any length of time, an airlock forms in the end of the stem and this will shorten their life. Always recut the stems at an angle and preferably underwater before replacing them in water — the angle cut will prevent the stalks sitting flat on the bottom of the vase thus inhibiting the take-up of water.

~ If you find your flowers wilting, try first recutting the stems and then submerging them completely in a bath of water. If the heads are still bent, wrap the whole flower tightly in plain paper and place the flowers, up to their necks, in a deep bucket of lukewarm water to which flower food has been added. This will also help to open up the flowers.

~ Floral preserver is commercially available from most florists or you can make your own. First, a little sugar will feed the flowers, allowing them to open and continue to grow in the vase. The sugar, however, is an ideal breeding ground for bacteria, so a little bleach should be added to stop the water turning smelly and slimy. Finally, you need to acidify the solution with a little vinegar in order to thin it down so that the flower can draw the food all the way up the stem to the head. The quantities will vary from variety to variety. Begin with a pinch and a few drops of each and experiment till you find the right recipe for your flowers and your environment.

~ Some flowers such as magnolias and water lilies are temperamental and can close up their blooms. Candle wax dropped into the middle of each flower will prevent this.

~ Some flowers such as gardenias begin turning brown rather quickly. You can retard this process by sprinkling the back of each bloom with a little salt.

Flowers for weddings

Weddings are a time when you can really go all out with flowers. Tone the shades and types of flowers in the house to those of the clothes of the wedding party.

~ Swag doorways with ivy garlands: cut the ivy as long as possible and wire it together in clumps using florist wire, twisting the strands a little as you go so that any additional flowers will be held in place without extra wire. You can even hang blooms from the middle of the arches, or use satin or tulle bows. Make sure you spray garlands with water to keep them fresh until the guests arrive.

~ You may choose to have a floral arrangement on each table — a round one works best on round tables, or try a garland down the middle of long tables to match the door arrangement. Add a special twist by including original items in the arrangements such as limes or bright red chilies. Use floral foam to hold the flowers in place: soak it first in water, but don't force it under or the middle of the foam will remain dry. If the weather is particularly hot, you can purchase small vials with rubber tops from your florist. Fill them with water and push individual stems through the top. The flowers will keep as long as the water lasts.

~ Place a flower on each guest's napkin as a memento of the day.

~ Decorate the cake with fresh flowers, and the knife with a few blooms and a bow.

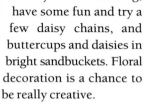

to accentuate a table's length. A mass of blooms might be perfect in the middle of a round or square table, and individual posies are charming gestures to each guest as well as a decorative link between the settings. If your dining room contains a sideboard, you may want to display a taller arrangment there to echo the table's floral piece. Remember to arrange the table flowers so that your guests can easily see each other and converse. Beware heavily scented flowers that may drown the aromas of the dishes. The flowers are there to add to the ambience, not to overpower the food and intimidate the guests.

An evening cocktail party with your guests in formal wear should feature sophisticated flowers. All white works very well at night, with large simple blooms such as lilies and magnolias. On these occasions, you might also consider using a highly perfumed flower, such as tuberose or gardenia.

The charm of entertaining at home is the warm and welcoming ambience not found in restaurants and hotels. Your flowers should reflect this, so stay away from stiff, contrived arrangements unless your home is built and decorated in a complimentary style. Go for quality, style, simplicity, and flowers that are at their peak. Your florist can give you advice regarding what flowers to buy and when.

Use your imagination: experiment with unusual containers and combinations of flowers, vegetables, and fruit. Why not a line of low-growing herbs in terracotta pots? If it's a children's party that you are hosting, have some fun and try a few daisy chains, and buttercups and daisies in bright sandbuckets. Floral decoration is a chance to be really creative.

Making an ice bowl

Use either cold boiled water or still mineral water so that the ice does not become cloudy, and choose two glass or metal bowls sized so that one fits inside the other with at least a 1-inch (2.5-cm) gap in between.

Pour approximately 1 cup of water and a handful of pretty petals into the larger bowl, sit the smaller bowl inside, and weigh down with a heavy pan or other weight, then freeze. When frozen, add another cup of water and petals to the bowl and freeze again. Continue this process until the bowl is full. Although these steps are time consuming, it ensures the petals are evenly spaced throughout the bowl and don't just float to the top.

When completely frozen, carefully remove inner bowl. If removal is difficult, fill it quickly with hot water and drain. Remove the outer bowl, dipping in hot water if necessary. Place the ice bowl in freezer until required.

When serving, place the ice bowl on a platter, surround with fruits in season, and fill with a dessert or refreshment.

Choosing and serving wine

Whoever said "rules were made to be broken" could easily have had food and wine in mind. Although the first word most of us hear on the subject is "white wine with white meat; red with red", there are few immutable rules governing what wines should be served with what foods.

There are some guidelines worth noting. The first is to match like with like. Pair light wines with light foods and

strong with strong. A delicate meal such as steamed white-fleshed fish with steamed vegetables needs a delicate, dry, steely wine such as a white Bordeaux, an unwooded dry semillon, or a Chablis.

Spicy foods need spicy wines: a gewürztraminer with a Vietnamese salad, for example. Be careful with chili: all but a very modest amount can kill wine. With strong curry, beer is the only drink. Water may be cool, but the bubbles of beer and its bitterness are much better than water as fire-fighting weapons.

Another concern is vinegary food, such as salad with vinaigrette dressing or vinegar-marinated antipasto. This need not be a problem: simply eat the vinegary things without wine, and resume your imbibing afterwards. (This is not usually workable with chili because the recovery time after a direct-hit is much longer.)

Artichokes, asparagus, and eggs are considered incompatible with wine by some people, but others team them with sauvignon blanc, grassy semillons, and some rieslings.

Most red-meat dishes go well enough with most red wines: the match need not be very precise. But this is just a starting point, as many red wines go well with white meats and seafoods, depending on whether the food is marinated, and how it is cooked and sauced. I have often enjoyed char-grilled octopus with a lightly spicy chili-based sauce and washed it down with pinot noir. Or quail thrown on the barbecue and served up with pinot noir, Beaujolais, or one of the many light-bodied, carbonic-maceration "nouveau" style reds available would do well. Delicate pinot goes spectacularly with atlantic salmon, too.

The converse is also possible. A rich, complex chardonnay can go very happily with some lighter red-meat dishes, such as schnitzel or scalloppine, rabbit casseroled in white wine, or even lamb fillets pan-roasted and served with béarnaise or pesto.

The best food wines are the simple ones. This is why many "New World" white wines are difficult to pair with food. Modern winemakers tend to heighten fruit and "bigness", and big whites generally don't go well with food, fighting rather than complementing it. A simple, delicate, bone-dry white like a fresh semillon or a steely riesling, however, will go well with a wide range of food.

Sweet foods need sweet wines, but the sweetness of the wine must at least equal that of the dish, otherwise the wine will taste thin and acid. On the other hand, sweet wines don't have to have sweet food. Sauternes can be a fine partner to savory foods such as foie gras or liver pâté, and especially salty or blue cheeses like gorgonzola and roquefort.

Cheese and wine are words that roll off the tongue together. But all cheese does not go with all wines, as many people assume. Far from it. One noted cheesemaker found after research that a non-botrytised, very sweet wine blended from orange muscat and flora was the best general-purpose cheese wine, tasting good with a wide range of cheese types. Most sweet whites are good with cheeses, especially the blue types, the salty and pungent-tasting. Vintage and tawny port are excellent with stilton, gorgonzola and other blues, as are liqueur muscats and tokays and sweeter Madeiras.

It is common practise to serve a mixed plate of cheeses with red wine without much thought. But red wine — especially dry, tannic red—is not a good match for most cheeses. Notable exceptions are cheddar, brie, camembert, washed-rind cheeses such as munster, and especially grana and other mature, crumbly parmesans.

Perfect matches

Dry, premium sparkling wine — *smoked fish, caviar, fresh oysters, canapés.*

Dry sherry — *tapas, antipasto, hors d'oeuvres.*

Amontillado sherry — *consommé, meat and vegetable-based soup.*

Dry riesling — *fish, salads, quiches, vegetarian dishes, antipasto.*

Dry semillon — *oysters, scallops, shrimp, prawns, fish, sushi, sashimi, antipasto, salads, chicken.*

Aged dry riesling or semillon — *cured fish (e.g. trout, eel), terrines, salads, cold meats.*

Gewürztraminer — *liver pâtés, lightly spiced Asian food including gentle curries.*

Verdelho (dry) — *chicken, fish, yabbies or marron, vegetable dishes.*

Marsanne, viognier, Condrieu, white Hermitage — *lightly spiced Asian dishes, honey shrimp (prawns), poultry.*

Chardonnay, white Burgundy — *chicken, pasta, fish, crayfish, seafood, lighter veal and pork dishes, offal.*

Sauvignon blanc, Sancerre — *asparagus, salads, mussels, crab, goat's cheese.*

Chenin blanc, Loire dry whites — *fish, salads, vegetarian dishes.*

Muscat or frontignac (dry) — *aperitif*

Muscat or frontignac (sweet) — *fresh fruit.*

Rosé — *bouillabaisse, paella, cold meats, cured meats, antipasto, pasta, smoked fish.*

Pinot noir, red Burgundy — *all game birds, coq au vin, pork, veal, beef carpaccio, Asian foods (e.g. Peking duck), pasta, tuna.*

Cabernet sauvignon, Bordeaux — *lamb and mutton, venison, all red meats.*

Shiraz (syrah), Rhône Valley, Spanish and Italian full-bodied reds — *beef, rabbit, hare, liver, kidneys.*

Mature rich reds — *cheddar, brie, camembert, cassoulet, osso bucco, casseroles.*

Rich botrytis sweet whites — *rich desserts especially crème brulée, foie gras, pâté, duck liver, blue and salty cheeses.*

Vintage port — *fresh walnuts and pecans, dried fruit, stilton, gorgonzola, all blue cheeses.*

Tawny port, Oloroso sherry — *blue cheeses, parmesan, cheddar, dried friut, nuts.*

Liqueur muscat or tokay, Malmsey — *fruit cake, chocolate desserts, blue cheeses, dried fruit.*

A long, late breakfast

Serves 6-8

Fruit Platter

Eggs with Salmon Roe

~

Choice of

Sublime Starter

Oat, Nut, and Fruit Pancakes with Poached Blood Plums & Creamy Yoghurt

Quinoa Pudding

~

Choice of

Home-Made Breads
Seed Loaf ~ Dunkirk Bread ~ Irish Tea Brack
Served with Orange, Apple, and Ginger Marmalade
& Lime and Lemon Marmalade

~

Fresh Fruit Frappés
Mango and Berry ~ Honeydew

a wedge of melon and a glass of orange juice on a summer morning—that's my idea of heaven. Or perhaps a plate of white peaches cut in the shape of a crescent moon, or a pink papaya cut in half, with fresh lime squeezed over it.

An even greater luxury is to be served this repast in bed, which at our house may happen only once a year. For most of us these days, leisurely breakfasts are out of the question. A gulp of juice, a mouthful of cereal, a swig of coffee or tea, and we're out the door to find our way through another day of work. We even seem to run out of time to sit down at the table and glance at each other over the tops of newspapers. Perhaps it is only when we're on vacation or on the occasional weekend that we can find time to indulge in a long, late breakfast.

The breakfast tradition

Most of us usually resist anything too fancy for breakfast, or too elaborate. Long gone are the days of groaning sideboards when servants would supply and replenish food from 8 am till 2 pm. Gone too are the days—and appetites—of Queen Elizabeth I. As MFK Fisher observes in The Art of Eating, *"the Queen, God be thanked, paid no attention to the new-style finicking, and made her first meal of the day light but sustaining: butter, bread (brown to stay in the stomach longer and more wholesomely than white), a stew of mutton, a joint of beef, one of veal, some rabbits in a pie, chickens, and fruits, with beer and wine to wash all down in really hygienic fashion." She wouldn't have had time to work it off at the gym afterward—lunch in those days was served at 11 am.*

The word "breakfast" once meant the first food eaten after waking to "break" the "fast" of a long night spent without food. Some of us are good "morning people" and welcome a substantial breakfast, even though these have become unfashionable in our health-conscious times. Others feel more fragile and need time to recover from the small daily trauma of waking up and getting out of bed.

Different countries have different traditions: the British still enjoy cereal and milk followed by bacon and eggs, and toast and jam, whereas the French just across the Channel partake of a croissant or roll and a cup of coffee. Americans have made fruit indispensable at the breakfast table, and it is to Dr Bircher-Benner that we can be grateful for the introduction of the raw fruit porridge, muesli, or granola as it is also called. Invented by him at his Zurich clinic for a patient unable to digest cooked food, this cereal has become an essential breakfast item for millions. Commercially-

made cereal, however, is a world apart from the home-made version, which is luxurious in the true sense of the word. Bircher-Benner's original recipe called for oats, sweetened condensed milk, grated apple, a little lemon juice, and chopped nuts, and was really more of a pudding than a breakfast food.

No matter what the tradition, however, nutritionists consider it essential to eat a wholesome breakfast each day. A good breakfast renews energy levels and helps your metabolism to get going. And treating yourself and your friends to a long, late breakfast renews the spirit.

Menu suggestions

Interesting and unusual home-baked breads are always a welcome addition to the breakfast table, as are home-made preserves and marmalades. For cooked breakfasts, even in these cholesterol conscious times, it's still hard to go past egg dishes. In the past, all sorts of different eggs were eaten—duck, turkey, seagull, swan, goose, and hen's eggs (which weren't as large as ours today). Peacock eggs were considered a luxury and kept for feasts. When made properly, there is nothing more delicious than eggs benedict, a savory omelette, or the creamy lusciousness of eggs florentine.

Fresh orange juice is a wonderful treat. Choose juicy oranges in season (valencias are excellent for juice), allowing 2-3 per person, depending on size. Cut the oranges in half and hand-squeeze—don't worry about a few pips sneaking in, as they give the juice a home-made look.

This menu

For this breakfast menu, we have kept to simple, good fare—food which can either be prepared the day before or which requires a little last-minute work in the kitchen. For example, the breads can be made well ahead and kept frozen. Take them out of the freezer the night before. Marmalades and preserves can also be prepared well in advance. Last-minute shopping will involve buying fresh eggs, salmon roe, and fruit, although these too can be bought the day before.

Because breakfast is such a casual, friendly affair, your guests can be with you in the kitchen while you boil the eggs and make the frappés and tea. Or you may wish to prepare as much as possible in advance. If so, keep toast warm by

wrapping it in a clean cloth—you can present the wrapped bundle at the table in an attractive basket. Make freshly brewed coffee by whichever means you prefer—expresso, plunger, filter. Keep it warm beforehand in a large thermos, and use another thermos to keep heated milk warm if you are serving it with coffee or cereal. Chafing dishes can be used on the table to keep items warm while you eat. If guests have stayed overnight, they might help set the table and sideboard. Otherwise, these can be set up the day before, so that you are free of those tasks.

The table for our menu has been laid casually but with all the essentials—a bowl for cereal or quinoa, a large plate for the pancakes or fresh fruit, a side plate for the toast and egg, and a glass for the juice or frappé. Set out some of the dishes on a sideboard or buffet and let the guests serve themselves. The fruit can be cut and laid out on a platter, and the cereal presented in a large bowl. Bring the eggs to the table and offer them individually.

Make this breakfast the start of a long, lazy day. If you start around 10 am, you'll have plenty of time afterward to read, or go for a long walk, or do whatever you like. Provide your guests with a selection of newspapers and games after they have finished eating.

The tradition of brunch varies in that it starts later and usually includes alcohol (in the form of champagne) and more substantial dishes. Breakfast, somehow, seems more intimate, a chance to entertain friends in a leisurely way.

eggs with salmon roe

Fruit platter

To begin, offer a selection of fruit in season. You might like to choose from pink grapefruit, honeydew melon, rockmelon (cantaloupe), pink pawpaw (papaya), or mangoes.

Halve the grapefruit, loosen flesh from the pith, and slice flesh into eating segments with a small sharp knife. Slice melons into wedges. Cut pawpaw into halves or wedges, depending on size. Offer wedges of lime or lemon to squeeze on the rockmelon and pawpaw. Slice cheeks off mangoes and cut flesh into squares through to the skin, then flip open to form a hedgehog pattern.

Eggs with salmon roe

Always use the freshest eggs available and have them at room temperature. Fresh eggs feel heavy and, when cracked open, have a rounded yolk, and a firm white. Allow 1 egg per person.

large eggs
unsalted butter, softened
salmon roe

Place eggs carefully in a saucepan and cover with warm water. Bring to a boil and simmer gently for 3–4 minutes. Remove from water, open up the tops, scoop out a little of the egg, dab with some butter, and heap with a teaspoon or two of "golden caviar" (salmon roe).

Sublime starter

Serves 5-6

This is a wickedly rich version of the original Bircher cereal. It is best prepared on the morning of your breakfast, but you can make it up the night before and keep chilled and covered in the refrigerator.

8 fl oz/250 ml thickened or whipping cream
8 fl oz/250 ml plain yogurt
8 oz/250 g mixed fresh or frozen berries (raspberries, blackberries, blueberries, strawberries)
1 1/2 oz/45 g shredded coconut

1 1/2 oz/45 g honey, or to taste
1 1/2 oz/45 g chopped dried figs
1 1/2 oz/45 g chopped dried dates
1 1/2 oz/45 g chopped dried apricots
1 1/2 oz/45 g sultanas (golden raisins)
1 1/2 oz/45 g broken walnuts or pecans

*W*hisk cream until it falls in soft folds. Place in a large bowl and stir through yogurt. Add all remaining ingredients, stirring well to combine. Keep covered in refrigerator. Stir again just before serving.

sublime starter

Oat, nut, and fruit pancakes

Makes 12 pancakes
Start the preparation for these the night before.

6 oz/185 g rolled oats
2 oz/60 g finely ground blanched almonds
4 fl oz/125 ml hot water
2 teaspoons honey
6 fl oz/185 ml fresh orange juice
2 teaspoons vegetable oil
2 tablespoons sultanas (golden raisins)
1 egg, beaten with 2 tablespoons water
vegetable oil for frying

*P*rocess oats in a food processor until lightly cracked. Blend almonds with hot water and honey until thick and creamy. Stir into oats with juice and oil to make a smooth batter. Add sultanas and leave to stand overnight at room temperature.

When ready to make pancakes, add beaten egg. If mixture is too thick, add a little more water or fruit juice.

Heat a heavy frying pan and oil lightly with a paper towel. Spoon in the batter, 2 tablespoonsful at a time. Turn when bubbles appear on the surface. Cook until golden on both sides.

Serve immediately with poached blood plums (see recipe below) and creamy yogurt.

Poached blood plums

32 fl oz/1 l water
7 oz/200 g sugar
peel of 1/2 orange
peel of 1/2 lemon
1 cinnamon stick
2 lb/1 kg blood plums, halved and pitted

*M*ake a sugar syrup by bringing water, sugar, citrus peel, and cinnamon stick to a boil in a large saucepan, stirring to dissolve sugar. Add plums, and poach gently for 8–10 minutes, or until softened. Remove from heat and let the plums sit in the syrup.

Quinoa pudding

Further information about quinoa and kuzu can be found in the glossary on page 203.

7 oz/200 g quinoa, washed and drained
20 fl oz/625 ml vanilla soy milk
pinch salt
2 tablespoons sesame paste (tahini)
3 tablespoons maple syrup
1 tablespoon arrowroot or kuzu, dissolved in
 1 tablespoon water
3 oz/90 g dried figs, chopped
a few extra dried or fresh figs, roughly chopped, to garnish

*B*ring quinoa and soy milk to a boil in a saucepan. Cover and simmer for 20 minutes. Add salt, sesame paste, and maple syrup. Add arrowroot, and stir until mixture thickens. Cool a little, then stir in figs. Garnish with additional figs, and more soy milk, if liked.

oat, nut, and fruit pancakes, poached blood plums, creamy yogurt

quinoa pudding

Seed loaf

A stoneground wholemeal (wholewheat) flour is recommended for this loaf. Keep in mind that different flours have different levels of absorbency so the quantity may vary slightly.

about 14 oz/440 g plain (all-purpose) flour
3 oz/90 g cracked wheat (bulghur)
1 sachet (1/4 oz/7 g) dry yeast
1/2 teaspoon sea salt
2 fl oz/60 ml maple syrup or molasses
2 fl oz/60 ml vegetable oil
10 fl oz/300 ml orange juice
5 oz/150 g toasted sunflower seeds
1 oz/30 g toasted sesame seeds
1 oz/30 g poppy seeds
extra sunflower or poppy seeds, for top

Place flour, cracked wheat, dry yeast, and salt in a large bowl, and combine well. Make a hole in the middle and pour in maple syrup, oil, and juice. With a wooden spoon, combine to make a dough, adding more flour or juice if required. Transfer to a floured bench and knead until smooth and shiny. If the dough is sticky, knead in a little more flour.

Shape dough into a ball and place in a lightly oiled bowl. Cover, and leave in a warm place until doubled in bulk, about 1–1 1/2 hours (length of time will depend on the temperature).

Remove from bowl and punch down. Knead in seeds (they will spill out, but just keep kneading them back in).

Shape into two loaves. Place on a lightly greased baking sheet and leave to rise for another 1–1 1/2 hours or until doubled again in bulk.

Preheat oven to 375 °F (190°C/Gas 5). Lightly sprinkle tops with extra seeds and bake 30–35 minutes or until lightly browned and sounding hollow when tapped. Remove from oven and cool on an oven rack.

Dunkirk bread

This much-loved classic is very easy to make.

12 oz/375 g self-raising flour
3 2/3 oz/110 g unprocessed bran
2 1/2 oz/75 g whole (full-cream) powdered milk
pinch salt
about 16 fl oz/500 ml water

Preheat oven to 400°F (200°C/Gas 6). Lightly grease a bread or loaf pan with butter.

Place all dry ingredients in a bowl and stir well to combine. Make a hole in the middle and pour in some of the water, gradually stirring in the flour mixture from the sides. Add enough water to make a paste and beat well with an electric beater for a few minutes to aerate.

Spoon mixture into prepared pan and bake for 1 hour. Remove from oven and turn out onto a rack to cool.

Irish tea brack

1 lb/500 g plain (all-purpose) flour
1/2 teaspoon cinnamon
1/2 teaspoon nutmeg
pinch salt
1 1/2 sachets (1/3 oz/10 g) dry yeast
3 tablespoons sugar
2 oz/60 g butter
2 eggs, beaten
10 fl oz/300 ml warm milk
5 oz/150 g sultanas (golden raisins)
5 oz/150 g currants
3 oz/90 g mixed peel
2 tablespoons boiling water

Sift together flour, spices, and salt. Stir in yeast and 2 tablespoons sugar; mix to combine. Rub in butter until mixture resembles breadcrumbs. Make a well in the middle and add eggs and milk. Beat well with a wooden spoon, then fold in fruits. Cover with plastic wrap and a cloth, and leave in a warm place for about 1 hour or until doubled in bulk (the time will depend on temperature).

Lightly grease a 9-in (23-cm) cake pan. Preheat oven to 375°F (190°C/Gas 5).

Turn dough into prepared pan and bake for about 1 hour, until a skewer inserted in the middle comes out clean. Remove from oven and glaze with a syrup, made by dissolving the remaining tablespoon sugar in the boiling water. Return to oven for a further 3 minutes. Cool on a wire tray.

from left to right: Irish tea brack, Dunkirk bread, seed loaf

Orange, apple, and ginger marmalade

Makes 10 8-fl oz (250-ml) jars

A handy hint to enable the sugar to dissolve more easily: warm it in the oven. Spread out on one or two baking trays in a moderate oven for 10 minutes.

5 large oranges, scrubbed and dried well
96 fl oz/3 l water, for oranges
3 lb/1.5 kg cooking apples, peeled, cored, and sliced
5 fl oz/150 ml water, for apples
5 lb/2.5 kg sugar
4 oz/125 g preserved ginger, chopped
juice of 1 lemon

Using a vegetable peeler, remove zest from oranges, and shred finely. Discard pith and pips. Chop flesh, reserving juices. Pour water into a large pan, and add orange zest, chopped orange flesh, and juices. Simmer for 1½ hours.

In a large pan, simmer apples gently in water until soft. Add to oranges, together with sugar, and bring to a boil, stirring until sugar has dissolved. Add ginger and lemon juice. Boil rapidly until the mixture gels, about 30 minutes.

Remove from heat and let stand 15 minutes. Ladle into sterile jars (easiest with a wide-necked funnel). Cover and seal when cool. Store in a cool, dry place.

Lime and lemon marmalade

Makes 5 8-fl oz (250-ml) jars

7 medium limes, scrubbed and dried well
3 medium lemons, scrubbed and dried well
80 fl oz/2.5 l cold water
about 2 lb/1 kg sugar

Using a vegetable peeler, remove zest from fruit as finely as possible and cut into thin shreds. Remove pith (white flesh) from fruit and put it into a cheesecloth (muslin) bag. Tie bag up with string. Chop flesh as finely as possible, reserving all the juice.

Place flesh, juice, zest, bag of pith, and water into a large pan. Bring to a boil and simmer over low heat until liquid is reduced by half. Discard the bag.

Measure the pulp and return to the pan with an equal volume of sugar, cup for cup. Bring to a boil, stirring occasionally to dissolve sugar. When sugar has dissolved, let boil without stirring until mixture gels, about 30 minutes. Skim off any scum as it forms.

Remove from heat and allow to stand for 5 minutes. Stir, then bottle in sterile jars. Cover and seal when cool. Store in a cool, dry place.

Fresh fruit frappés

You can make these fabulous drinks from most fruits: try white peach with raspberry; pawpaw (papaya), pineapple, and rockmelon (cantaloupe); pineapple and mint; fresh lime juice with a little egg white for fluffiness. Using the example below as a guide, make up your own delicious combinations. The portions below serve 2 people.

Make the sugar syrup by mixing together equal volumes of caster (superfine) sugar and boiling water; try 8 oz / 250 g of sugar to 8 fl oz / 250 ml water. Stir well until dissolved, then let cool. You may decide to omit the sugar syrup altogether if the fruits are sweet.

Mango and berry frappé

1 large mango, flesh only
3 oz/90 g fresh raspberries or strawberries
1 cup crushed ice
3¹/₂ fl oz/100 ml sugar syrup or to taste

Place all ingredients in a blender or food processor and purée until smooth.

Honeydew frappé

²/₃ honeydew melon, peeled, seeded, and cut in chunks
few leaves fresh mint
1¹/₂ cups crushed ice
small knob ginger, peeled
3¹/₂ fl oz/100 ml sugar syrup or to taste

Place all ingredients in a blender or food processor and purée until smooth.

A gourmet barbecue

A gourmet barbecue

Serves 14

A Selection of Dips served with Crudités and Crusty Bread

Skordalia ~ Eggplant Dip ~ Tzatziki

Brandade de Morue served with Triangles of Toast

~

Marinated Baby Octopus

Barbounia

Horiatiki Salad

~

Butterfly Leg of Lamb

Green Beans with Potatoes and Mint

Barbecued Vegetables

~

Greek Almond and Walnut Syrup Cake with Cream or Natural Yoghurt

Toula's Melomacarona

Coffee or Tea

Hondeydew Melon Ice & Watermelon Wedges

*t*he smells of a barbecue are irresistible. The very word evokes warm days, balmy evenings, and the wonderful carefree feeling of summer.

Barbecues are perfect for casual entertaining. Usually, they are less work because guests are willing to help. I have also discovered over the years that it is important to provide plenty of food, more than you normally would for an indoor meal. You may have noticed that appetites seem larger when you entertain outdoors. A platter of crudités with some interesting dips will be appreciated as will good fresh bread, fresh fruit, and bowls of olives and nuts. Fresh salads made from vegetables in season are both good to pick at and use as accompaniments to the main meal. Any food you broil or grill in the kitchen can be barbecued. If you don't normally barbecue vegetables, do try as they can make an interesting addition to the meal.

Marinating

Marinades can be used extensively to improve the taste of food and to tenderize it before cooking. There are many types of marinades you can create, and the ingredients you use will be determined by the style of your barbecue. If, like this menu, it's a Mediterranean-style barbecue you are aiming for, use ingredients local to the area, such as olive oil, garlic, rosemary, thyme, and mint. If it's more in the Asian style, use ingredients such as soy sauce, honey, freshly grated ginger, fresh coriander leaves (cilantro), and lemongrass.

An easy marinating method is to place the meat, fish, or poultry in a plastic bag along with the marinade. The food is then covered and easily turned inside the bag without mess. Alternatively, use a glass or ceramic dish and cover with plastic wrap—metal will taint the food. Turn the food a few times so that it absorbs the marinade. Score a whole fish to assist absorption. Before barbecuing, drain off the marinade into a bowl or jug and brush it over the food as it cooks—if you pour it, the fire will flare-up and you will end up with burned meat.

Equipment and fuel

There is a lot of well-designed barbecue equipment available, from the simplest charcoal-fueled braziers to more elaborate, vented ones. The latter have covers and some come with motorized rotisseries, kebab holders, and even built-in thermometers so that you can cook cakes in them. Which barbecue you choose will depend on how much money you have to spend and whether you want a portable or fixed type. Gas and electric versions are also available if you prefer them to the coal and wood-burning varieties, but remember you will need access to an energy source if using these.

Your barbecue will only be as good as your fire. You don't want leaping flames. What you need are glowing coals covered with white ash. Charcoal and heat beads are excellent because they burn for a long time and distribute the heat evenly. Shape them into a mound and light with three or four firestarters—make sure these do not contain petroleum by-products as they alter, rather than enhance, the taste of the food. Allow 40-60 minutes for the coals to turn to whitish-gray embers, then spread them out evenly and begin cooking. If you need to increase the heat, push the coals closer together—for a lower heat, just spread them out again. If using a covered barbecue, read the instruction manual carefully. With this kind of barbecue, many dishes are best cooked indirectly over a drip tray with fuel moved to the sides.

The type of fuel you use will greatly affect the taste of the food. If there is plenty of dry wood available, you can build your fire with that. Start with scrunched-up paper, dry twigs, leaves, and kindling, gradually adding larger pieces of wood as you go. It will take at least an hour for the wood to be covered with ash and glowing, so allow plenty of time beforehand. Resinous woods such as pine will taint food, whereas oak is ideal. Experiment with different types of aromatic woods: hickory, for example, imparts a sweet, mellow taste to the food, as do fresh herbs thrown directly onto the coals. It's a good idea to soak the herbs for half an hour beforehand to avoid burning. Grape vine clippings added five minutes before you begin cooking add a delicious and distinctive element. Ensure the table is a long way from the fire so that guests are not disturbed by excessive smoke.

If possible, try to have two different barbecues going— one to cook the meat and vegetables, the other for the seafood, as this prevents the tastes getting mixed up. Asking a friend to bring a portable one is a viable solution.

Cooking hints

Before cooking, make sure the grill or cooking surface is clean, then brush with oil to prevent sticking, or trim some of the fat from the meat and use it for greasing. To turn food over, use a pair of long tongs, as forks will puncture the food and you will lose precious juices. A pair of long barbecue or oven mitts will also come in handy. Long-handed, wide metal spatulas are useful for turning fish, hamburgers, and eggs. A water spray is handy for dousing unwanted flames, and access to a hose or running water is important for safety.

Barbecue foods are often "wrapped" to retain moisture and impart a different taste. Vine leaves, banana leaves, and lemon leaves can be used as wrappings. Foil is the easiest (though less flavorful) method. If you use foil, place the food on the shiny side and face the dull side to the heat. Bring refrigerated food back to room temperature before

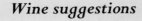

Wine suggestions

~ With *the octopus*: a dry white of spice and personality such as an Alsatian pinot gris or gewürztraminer, or a tangy sauvignon blanc from Sancerre or New Zealand.

~ With *the lamb*: A soft, spicy red such as Côtes-du-Rhône or a medium-bodied Australian Shiraz from the Barossa Valley.

~ Ouzo and water before the meal will contribute to the Mediterranean theme.

cooking, otherwise it may burn on the outside and be raw in the middle. Give thought to timing—for example, octopus won't take nearly as long to cook as a butterflied leg of lamb, so plan your schedule before starting. For this menu, cooking would proceed in the following order: lamb 20-25 minutes (plus another 10 minutes resting while you cook the vegetables), fish 8-10 minutes, capsicum (bell pepper) and eggplants (aubergine) 8 minutes, fennel 7-8 minutes, zucchini (courgettes) 5-6 minutes, and octopus 4-5 minutes.

This menu

When guests first arrive, and while the barbecue is heating up, serve drinks and crudités with one of the dips provided in this menu as well as the Brandade de Morue. It is served with toast, but the crudités can also be dipped into it. Serve the baby octopus next, and have the horiatiki salad in a bowl on the table. Cook the barbounia after the octopus and serve them next, remembering that not everyone is likely to eat fish. The main course is lamb, vegetables, and green beans, finishing with a choice of cake and/or biscuits for dessert. A crusty Italian-style bread should accompany the meal, and a selection of condiments can be offered: lemons for the fish, olive oil and vinegar for the salad, kumquats in syrup for dessert. Olives make a tasty nibble, especially the Kalamata variety. Try marinating them in olive oil, herbs, garlic, and a little chili.

Outdoor eating should be casual and simple. Add interest to the eating area with just a few intriguing elements: fresh herbs in pots, fresh lemons with their leaves, a handmade basket, or cherry tomatoes strung together with needle and thread and hung from a tree.

skordalia

Appetizers are good way to kick off your barbecue. Most people expect only a main course, so a few nibbles beforehand come as a surprise. Besides, once that barbecue is up and firing, they can help take the edge off hunger. Serve one, two, or more of the dips with crudités and/or fresh crusty bread.

Crudités

1 bunch celery, cut into 3-in/7.5-cm lengths
1 bunch scallions (green onions), cut into 3-in/7.5-cm lengths
2 bunches radishes, trimmed
iced water
4–6 red onions, peeled and cut into eighths

*A*fter preparing celery, scallions, and radishes, leave in iced water until just before serving. To serve, present the crudités on a platter with one or two of the following tasty dips.

Skordalia

This pungent garlic dip (skordo means "garlic" in Greek) is usually made with mashed potatoes and bread. In this version, based on a recipe of Michael Field's, ground almonds are used instead of potato. Make sure ingredients are at room temperature before you start.

3 egg yolks
1 tablespoon white wine vinegar
1 teaspoon salt
4 garlic cloves, peeled and crushed
2 tablespoons lemon juice
16 fl oz/500 ml olive oil
3 tablespoons fresh breadcrumbs
3 tablespoons blanched ground almonds
2 tablespoons finely chopped parsley
zest of 1 lemon, finely chopped

*P*rocess yolks, vinegar, salt, garlic, and lemon juice in a food processor. After a few seconds, pour in oil, drop by drop at first, then gradually more quickly. When the mayonnaise is thick, spoon into another bowl and gently stir in the remaining ingredients. Taste, and adjust seasoning and lemon juice if needed.

brandade de morue

Eggplant dip

2 lb/1 kg medium eggplants (aubergines)
2–3 ripe tomatoes, peeled and chopped
2 tablespoons chopped fresh parsley
1 tablespoon chopped fresh oregano or 1 teaspoon dried
3–4 fl oz/90–125 ml olive oil
about 6 tablespoons lemon juice or red wine vinegar

*P*reheat oven to 375°F (190°C/Gas 5). Prick eggplants with a fork. Bake whole on a lightly greased tray until they are soft.

Scoop out the eggplant pulp, placing it in a food processor or blender. Add all remaining ingredients except lemon juice. Purée. Work quickly whilst eggplant is still hot, as it starts to brown on contact with air. Stir in desired amount of lemon juice, tasting as you do, to make sure the balance is right. Spoon into a serving bowl.

Tzatziki

16 fl oz/500 ml creamy plain yogurt
1 medium cucumber, peeled and finely chopped
2 cloves garlic, crushed
1 tablespoon white vinegar
few sprigs fresh mint, chopped
few sprigs fresh dill, chopped
pinch salt
olive oil

*L*et yogurt drip through a sieve into a bowl; this should take about ¹/₂ hour. Squeeze cucumber in a piece of cheesecloth (muslin) to remove excess moisture, then mix into yogurt. Add garlic, vinegar, and herbs. Season to taste. Drizzle with olive oil before serving.

Brandade de morue

2 lb/1 kg dried salt cod
2–3 cloves garlic, crushed
6 fl oz/180 ml olive oil, warmed
4 fl oz/125 ml milk, warmed
1 potato, cooked in its skin and mashed, optional
black olives for garnish

*S*oak fish for 24 hours in cold water, changing water a few times. Drain and wash well. Place in a large saucepan of cold water and bring slowly to a simmer (the water should just shudder). Cook for 10 minutes, remove from heat, and leave in the cooking water for another 10 minutes.

Remove fish from water and take off all skin and bones. Place fish in a saucepan with garlic over low heat. Pound well with the end of a rolling pin or pestle. Add olive oil and milk little by little, stirring constantly to make a smooth cream. Do not let the mixture boil. There may still be some shreds of fish still in the dish, but that is characteristic. You can use a blender or food processor at this stage if you want a smoother purée.

If the mixture remains soft and fluid, mix in enough mashed potato to attain the desired consistency.

Pile the mixture into a mound on a serving dish and decorate with black olives. Serve with triangles of toast.

Marinated baby octopus

In Greece, octopus is beaten on the rocks by fishermen to tenderize it. In large commercial fish markets, tenderizing often takes place in a cement mixer. Choose baby octopus of the same size and be sure to check that they have been tenderized.

3 lb/1.5 kg baby octopus
6 fl oz/180 ml olive oil
3 fl oz/90 ml lemon juice
3 cloves garlic, crushed
1 bunch fresh mint, chopped

Prepare octopus by holding the head firmly and cutting through the flesh below the eyes. Pick up the tentacles and, with your index finger underneath, push out the beak (or mouth), and discard. Turn the heads inside out and remove all organs. Alternatively, cut through back of head, and clean. Cut into pieces or leave whole.

Marinate the octopus in a mixture of oil, lemon juice, garlic, and mint for 3–4 hours.

Cook over hot coals for 4–5 minutes, depending on size.

marinated baby octupus

55

barbounia

Barbounia

In Greece, this sweet, mellow fish is known as barbounia, in France as rouget de roche, in Italy as triglia, and to the English-speaking world as red mullet. They are considered a delicacy by many Mediterranean people and are particularly good barbecued. You can use other fish in this recipe—small bream and snapper work well. Care should be taken when eating, however, as the fish have many small bones.

20 vine (grape) leaves, either fresh or preserved
olive oil
10 small barbounia (red mullet), cleaned and scaled
salt and freshly ground black pepper
fennel tops, soaked in water for 1/2 hour

Blanch fresh leaves in boiling water for 2–3 minutes, drain, and pat dry. Trim any tough stems. If using leaves in brine, rinse in cold water, drain, and dry. Lightly brush the leaves with olive oil.

Wipe fish dry and sprinkle the cavity with salt and pepper. Place each fish on two overlapping leaves, roll up, tucking in the sides, and secure with string.

Just before barbecuing, throw the fennel tops onto the hot coals. Place fish onto hot oiled grill and cook for about 4–5 minutes on each side, depending on size.

Horiatiki salad

Otherwise known as "village salad".

4 firm ripe tomatoes, cut in wedges
1 cucumber, peeled, cut in half and sliced
1 green capsicum (bell pepper), seeds removed
   and sliced in rings
1 onion, sliced in thin rings
16–20 black Greek olives
4 oz/125 g feta cheese, broken or cubed
small bunch of parsley, chopped

For the dressing
4 tablespoons olive oil
1 tablespoon vinegar
1 teaspoon dried oregano or marjoram
salt and freshly ground black pepper

Place all the salad ingredients in a bowl and toss well, arranging in a decorative fashion. Mix together dressing ingredients in a jar and shake well. Pour over the salad just before serving.

Green beans with potatoes and mint

A simple yet delicious dish from the Peloponnese.

1 lb/500 g stringless green beans, topped, tailed,
    and cut into 2-in (5-cm) lengths
2 medium potatoes, peeled and sliced thinly
3 fl oz/90 ml olive oil
1 medium onion, sliced
1 14-oz/440-g can tomatoes
salt and freshly ground black pepper
2 tablespoons chopped fresh mint
additional fresh mint for garnish

*A*dd beans and potatoes to a saucepan of boiling water. As soon as water returns to a boil, remove from heat and drain vegetables.

In a large heavy frying pan, heat oil and cook onion until soft. Add beans, potatoes, and remaining ingredients, and cook until vegetables are tender, about 20 minutes.

If the sauce has not thickened, pour it into a small pan and reduce to about 1 cup (8 fl oz/250 ml), then combine with beans and potatoes in a serving bowl. Sprinkle with additional fresh mint and serve warm.

green beans with potatoes and mint

Butterfly leg of lamb

Ask the butcher to butterfly the lamb leg for you.

1 leg of lamb, about 3–4 lb/1.5–2 kg with bone, butterflied
1/2 cup (4 fl oz/125 ml) olive oil
1/4 cup (2 fl oz/60 ml) lemon juice
1/4 cup (2 fl oz/60 ml) dry white wine
3 teaspoons Dijon mustard
1 clove garlic, finely chopped
few strips lemon peel
2–3 teaspoons fresh thyme leaves

*C*ombine all ingredients and marinate the lamb in this mixture for a few hours or overnight. Drain, reserving the marinade.

Barbecue slowly over hot coals, keeping the lamb flat, and turning and basting frequently with the marinade. Cook for about 10–12 minutes on each side (this will depend on its thickness), and let rest for 10 minutes. Serve cut into juicy pink slices.

horiatiki salad

horiatiki salad, lamb with barbecued vegetables, green beans with potatoes and mint

Barbecued vegetables

There is really no set recipe for these, just a few guidelines. Use vegetables you have on hand, remembering to parboil or steam vegetables like potatoes, onions, corn, fennel, and sweet potatoes. Soak bamboo skewers in water for 30 minutes beforehand to prevent burning.

eggplants (aubergines)
red and/or yellow capsicums (bell peppers)
fennel bulbs
zucchini (courgettes)
olive oil
lemon juice
flaky sea salt and freshly ground black pepper

*E*ggplants: cut lengthwise into 1/3-in (8-mm) thick slices. Sprinkle each slice with salt and place in a colander. Let stand for 1/2 hour to disgorge any juices, rinse well under running water, and pat dry with paper towels.

Capsicums: cut into quarters, removing the membranes and seeds. Wash well and dry.
Fennel bulbs: trim tops and roots, and discard these and any old or unappealing outer layers. Cut lengthwise into 1/2-in (1-cm) thick slices and brush with a little lemon juice to prevent browning.
Zucchini: trim ends and cut in half lengthwise.

Brush vegetables with olive oil before barbecuing. Cook capsicum until the skin has blackened, then remove skin, and keep capsicum warm. For the other vegetables, cook, turning, until tender. If you want a cross-hatched effect, turn the vegetables 90° halfway through cooking and on both sides.

Eggplants take 8 minutes to cook, capsicum 8–10 minutes, fennel 7–8 minutes, and zucchini 5–6 minutes. Do not overcook them—the zucchini and fennel are best if served a little al dente.

Greek almond and walnut syrup cake

This quantity makes a generous cake. Serve with creamy natural yogurt or mounds of fresh cream.

11^1/$_2$ oz/350 g blanched ground almonds
5 oz/150 g walnuts, finely ground
3^1/$_2$ oz/100 g white breadcrumbs, made from day-old bread
1 teaspoon cinnamon
^{1}/$_2$ teaspoon ground cloves
8 eggs, separated
6^1/$_2$ oz/200 g caster (superfine) sugar
^{1}/$_2$ teaspoon vanilla essence/extract
finely grated zest of 1 large orange

For the syrup
24 fl oz/700 ml water
14 oz/400 g sugar
1 slice lemon, skin on

Preheat oven to 350°F (180°C/Gas 4). Butter and flour a springform pan, 12-in (30-cm) in diameter and 3-in (8-cm) deep.

Mix together nuts, breadcrumbs, and spices.

In another bowl, whisk egg yolks, sugar, and vanilla until very thick and pale. Add zest. Fold nut mixture into yolks. Whisk whites to a softly mounding snow. Pour over yolk and nut mixture, and fold in carefully. Pour the batter into the pan and bake for 45–50 minutes.

Meanwhile, make syrup by combining ingredients in a saucepan. Bring to a boil, making sure sugar dissolves, and boil for 10 minutes.

As soon as cake is removed from oven, pour syrup over it. Let cool in pan, then remove springform.

greek almond and walnut syrup cake

honeydew melon ice

Toula's melomacarona

This recipe makes about 40 wonderful, traditional Greek honey biscuits.

4 fl oz/125 ml light olive oil
8 oz/250 g unsalted butter, softened
3 1/2 oz/100 g fine semolina
1/2 teaspoon cinnamon
1/2 teaspoon ground cloves
1/2 teaspoon finely grated orange zest
1/2 teaspoon finely grated lemon zest
1/2 teaspoon baking powder
2 fl oz/60 ml brandy
2 fl oz/60 ml sweet white wine
3 oz/90 g honey
about 1 lb/500 g self-raising flour
finely crushed walnuts

For the syrup
3 oz/90 g honey
8 fl oz/250 ml water
4 oz/125 g sugar
squeeze of lemon juice

Preheat oven to 350°F (180°C/Gas 4). Put all ingredients, except flour and walnuts, into a mixing bowl. Beat well for about 10 minutes until the mixture is white and smooth; this is best achieved with a strong electric mixer. Slowly add flour, working by hand, to make a smooth firm texture, adding extra flour if needed.

Break off small pieces of dough and shape with fingers into oval shapes weighing about 1 oz (30 g) each, about the size of a walnut. Place on greased trays and bake about 15 minutes, until golden brown. Cool on a cake rack.

Place all syrup ingredients into a saucepan and bring to a boil, making sure sugar dissolves completely.

When the biscuits are cold, dip individually into hot syrup (using tongs if required) and place on a large flat tray. Sprinkle with crushed walnuts and allow to cool.

Honeydew melon ice

As a refreshing finale, serve honeydew melon ice and wedges of fresh pink watermelon.

1 honeydew melon, about 3 lb/1.5 kg, halved, seeded, and peeled
7 oz/220 g sugar
16 fl oz/500 ml water
3–4 tablespoons lemon juice
sprigs of mint, for garnish

Purée melon flesh in a blender or food processor until smooth. There should be about 4 cups (32 fl oz/1 l) of purée.

Meanwhile, bring sugar and water to boil in a saucepan, making sure sugar dissolves. Remove from heat and cool.

Stir sugar syrup into melon purée, adding lemon juice to taste. Place in freezer trays in the freezer. When the mixture begins to set, remove and blend again. Re-freeze.

Remove from freezer 10–15 minutes before serving. Spoon into glasses or bowls. Garnish with a sprig of mint.

A picnic in the garden

A picnic in the garden

Serves 10-12

Stuffed Olives

**Crusty Italian Bread with Salami
and Assorted Cheeses**

Pasta 'n Cacciata

Frittata

Raw Zucchini Salad

Lemon Salad

Lamb in Parmesan Crumbs

Giardiniera

~

Fresh Peaches with Mascarpone

Apricot and Ricotta Tart

~

Fresh Lemonade

Coffee and Tea

a white cloth thrown on the lawn, some perfectly ripe warm peaches and nectarines and a glass or two of a refreshing drink... It is possible to catch glimpses of paradise.

Sometimes, it is even possible to create your very own paradise—as in this picnic in a garden. Even if you don't have your own Garden of Eden, you can create a wonderful setting with potted trees, shrubs, and flowers, and a rug and tablecloth.

Such an idyllic vision is captured in "Le déjeuner sur l'herbe" by the French Impressionist Claude Monet. There, in a sun-dappled glade in the forest of Fontainebleau, a group of people have gathered to partake of a picnic. A cloth has been spread over the forest floor and on it a pâté in a pastry crust, a roasted chicken, bottles of wine and a loaf of bread, peaches and pears and glasses and plates. The people are elegantly dressed in the style of the period and look relaxed and happy. The golds, greens, yellows, and whites uplift and delight, transporting you into a different world. In France, the joys of eating and cooking are celebrated, and in this life-like fragment, Monet has captured the pleasure of a picnic. It was probably from the French "pique nique" that the English word derived.

Elegant, well-planned picnics have always enchanted me. Sitting outdoors with a group of friends, the scents of the garden intermingling with the smells of delicious food and wine, is one of life's greatest joys. By definition, a picnic usually involves a journey. For this picnic, however, we have traveled only as far as the garden. A beautiful garden can be the most memorable of picnic spots, or you could go to a local park near your home.

Perfect picnic foods

A picnic can be as simple or as elaborate as you like. In days gone by, picnics were much more formal than the ones we have today. Wealthy people could go to great trouble and employ a cook, a chauffeur, and a waiter, use the best silver and tablecloths and serve a vast number of dishes such as pâté de foie gras, a whole poached salmon or trout, a rare roast beef, a terrine of wild rabbit and duck, cold jellies and trifles. Generally, because a picnic involves carrying food and equipment, the simpler the better.

For this picnic, peasant-style foods with a southern Italian emphasis have been chosen. In Sicily, this type of food, which can be eaten in the hand, is called rosticceria. It includes dishes such as pasta 'n cacciata, frittata, crusty Italian bread, and tasty giardiniera. Many Italian dishes seem almost made for picnics, and those featured in this menu are no exception.

We have avoided plastic containers, foil, and styrofoam cups. Plastic can taint food and, anyway, it is far from elegant. If you use real glasses and plates, you can enjoy their clinking along with the buzz of conversation, and sounds of the birds.

Part of the fun of a picnic lies in the shopping and preparation for it. Try to avoid delicate and cream-based foods. Mousse may melt in the heat and seafood could develop bacteria and spoil. Foods that crumble or fall apart are not practical for picnics. Meat on the bone, hard-boiled eggs, cheeses, bread, fresh fruit, and a home-baked cake are always good standbys. Insulated containers of hot water can be used for coffee and tea, and one full of ice is a welcome addition on a hot day.

Start your main preparation a day or two beforehand: the pasta 'n cacciata in this menu can be made the day before (it improves overnight), as can the frittata and the deep-fried olives. Giardiniera (mixed pickled vegetables) can be purchased from good specialty stores, but making your own is always preferable. If you decide to do so, you will need to start it a couple of weeks beforehand. We suggest you round out the meal with crusty Italian bread, a good salami, and assorted cheeses such as pecorino pepato and castel sardo.

Take along a rug or plastic sheet in case the ground is damp—which is surprisingly common. Throw a handsome tablecloth over the top and unpack your basket or hamper (if it has been packed in order of eating, this task will be easier). Present all the food at once, except the peaches and mascarpone, which should be kept in an insulated container until ready to serve. This spread gives a feeling of abundance and invites people to choose for themselves.

Checklist of things to remember

~ large plastic groundsheet or rug (additional ones may be needed on which people can recline)

~ large umbrella for shade

~ cushions and/or folding chairs

~ games and musical instruments for entertainment

~ tablecloth

~ napkins (when packing, wrap these individually around the glasses to keep the glasses safe)

~ cutlery

~ plates (including extra plates for presenting food)

~ corkscrew (if taking wine)

~ bottle opener

~ glasses (you may find tumblers the most stable on uneven ground—pack them in a separate basket from the food to avoid breakage)

~ sharp knife for cutting

~ chopping board for slicing bread and other food

~ cloth for cleaning and wiping

~ plastic bags for litter and recycling

~ insect repellent and sun protection cream

~ food cover to protect against insects

~ insulated containers for hot water, cold drinks, and ice

~ containers of milk and sugar for tea and coffee

~ instant coffee and tea bags

~ salt and pepper mills

~ mayonnaise or vinaigrette in a screwtop jar (if using)

~ olive oil and lemons for dressing

Wine suggestions

Continue the Italian theme with a delicate, refreshing dry white wine, perhaps one of the better makes of Soave from Italy's Veneto region.

Stuffed olives

These stuffed olives are fiddly but well worth the effort as they are delicious. Once made, store them in a covered container in the refrigerator.

2 tablespoons olive oil
8 oz/250 g lean round (topside) steak, finely minced (ground)
8 oz/250 g lean pork, finely minced (ground)
salt and pepper
½ teaspoon dried basil
1 small carrot, peeled
1 small onion, peeled
2 stalks celery
4 fl oz/125 ml dry white wine
2 eggs, beaten
handful freshly grated parmesan
pinch nutmeg
40 green jumbo olives, dried
4 oz/125 g plain (all-purpose) flour, seasoned with salt
*   and pepper*
3 eggs, beaten
5 oz /155 g dried breadcrumbs
oil for deep frying

Heat oil in a frying pan. Add meat and brown all over. Season to taste. Add basil.

Process carrot, onion, and celery in a food processor until finely chopped. Add to the meat. Pour in wine and simmer over low heat, stirring frequently, for 30 minutes until all the liquid has evaporated and oil is at the bottom. Remove from heat and let cool.

Stir in the 2 beaten eggs, parmesan, and nutmeg, mixing well to combine. Cover and refrigerate.

"Peel" each olive with a small paring knife, going around and around until you reach the stone, keeping the strip of olive intact—just like peeling an orange. Form the cold meat mixture into walnut-sized balls with your hands. Wrap one olive peeling around each ball, pressing the peel into the meat and enclosing the whole ball. Place on a tray and refrigerate for 1 hour.

Roll each ball in seasoned flour, then in remaining beaten eggs, and then in dried breadcrumbs. Heat oil to 350°F (180°C) and deep fry olives until golden.

Pasta 'n cacciata

This is actually a pasta cake in an eggplant (aubergine) shell. Once you've mastered the basic procedure, you can vary this dish endlessly. Chopped basil, parsley, and fresh chilies are nice additions, as are artichoke hearts and olives.

melted butter to prepare pan
dried breadcrumbs to prepare pan
2–3 medium eggplants (aubergines), about 12 oz/350 g each,
sliced thinly lengthwise
2 fl oz/60 ml olive oil
2 onions, chopped
2 cloves garlic, crushed
2 14-oz (410-g) cans peeled tomatoes, drained and chopped
salt and pepper
1 teaspoon dried oregano
5 oz/150 g button mushrooms (champignons), sliced
7 oz/200 g shelled peas, cooked
14 oz/400 g penne or rigatoni pasta
3 oz/90 g parmesan, freshly grated
8 oz/250 g grated mozzarella cheese
2 hard-boiled eggs, chopped

Preheat oven to 400°F (200°C/Gas 6). Brush a 9–10 in (23–25 cm) diameter cake pan with butter, and coat lightly with breadcrumbs.

Dry fry the eggplant slices in a hot frying pan, remove, and cool. Lay the slices, overlapping, around the bottom and sides of the cake pan in a pretty pattern.

Heat the oil in a frying pan and sauté onion and garlic until transparent. Add tomatoes, salt, pepper, and oregano, and cook for 15–20 minutes, until the oil begins to separate from the sauce. Add mushrooms and peas, and cook until tender. Let cool.

Cook the pasta in plenty of rapidly boiling salted water until al dente, about 8–9 minutes. Mix well through the cooled sauce; the sauce should go inside the pasta shells. Stir in the cheeses. Spoon half the mixture into the lined pan. Cover with the eggs, then spoon in remaining mixture, pressing down well with your hands. Cover with foil. Bake for 20–25 minutes, remove foil, and let cool.

Refrigerate for 1 hour. With a spatula gently ease pasta cake away from sides of pan and onto a serving plate.

pasta 'n cacciata, raw zucchini salad, giardiniera

frittata

Frittata

Try to use the dark-green outer leaves of the lettuce when preparing this frittata.

3 tablespoons olive oil
2 medium potatoes, peeled and diced
5 oz/150 g pancetta or bacon, finely diced
8 oz/250 g freshly shelled peas
8–10 lettuce leaves, shredded
8 fl oz/250 ml chicken stock
6 large eggs, beaten
handful freshly grated parmesan
handful chopped basil
salt and pepper

Heat 1¹/₂ tablespoons oil in a frying pan. Sauté potatoes and pancetta until potato is lightly browned. Add peas, lettuce, and stock. Bring to a boil then simmer until potatoes and peas are tender and the stock is absorbed.

In a large mixing bowl combine beaten eggs, parmesan, and basil, and season to taste. Add potato mixture to eggs.

Heat remaining oil in a large frying pan, then pour in egg and potato mixture. Cook gently over low heat until eggs are set, about 15 minutes. Invert onto a plate and slide frittata back into pan to brown the other side. Alternatively, brown under a hot grill (broiler).

Serve cold, sliced into wedges.

Raw zucchini salad

1 lb/500 g young zucchini (courgettes), washed, well dried,
*   and cut thinly into round slices*
3 tablespoons good-quality olive oil
1¹/₂ tablespoons freshly squeezed lemon juice
salt to taste
chopped fresh mint

Chill zucchini. Just before serving, dress with oil and lemon juice. Season with salt and scatter with mint.

Lemon salad

In Sicily, lemons are picked fresh from the tree, peeled, and eaten with a pinch of salt. Sometimes the pulp is scooped out and made into a salad by tossing it with olive oil, salt, and olives. Try to find sweetish lemons, like Meyer. You'll find this salad is very cleansing to the palate.

6 lemons
about 3 tablespoons good-quality olive oil
salt and freshly ground black pepper
handful chopped fresh parsley
handful wrinkled black olives

Remove the peel and most of the pith from the lemons, then coarsely chop remaining pith and flesh, removing any seeds. Place in a bowl and toss with olive oil, salt, pepper, and parsley. Garnish with olives.

Lamb in parmesan crumbs

Allow one piece for light eaters and two for those with larger appetites. There's only a mouthful of meat in each piece.

10–15 lamb loin cutlets (chops)
3 oz/90 g all-purpose (plain) flour, seasoned with salt
*   and cayenne pepper*
2 eggs, lightly beaten
3 oz/90 g fresh white breadcrumbs
1¹/₂ oz/45 g freshly grated parmesan
light olive oil for frying
sea salt
lemon wedges

Roll lamb in seasoned flour, then eggs, and finally in a mixture of breadcrumbs and cheese.
  Heat oil in a frying pan on medium heat and fry lamb for 3–4 minutes on each side until golden. Drain on paper towels. Serve with sea salt and a wedge of lemon.

stuffed olives, lamb in parmesan crumbs, giardiniera

Giardiniera

You will need only 4 cups (32 fl oz/1 l) of pickle for this picnic, although this recipe makes 3 times that much. You can keep the remainder in jars in the pantry for several months. Store in the refrigerator once opened.

For the pickling solution
56 fl oz/1.75 l white wine vinegar or apple cider vinegar
8 fl oz/250 ml dry white wine
3¹/2 oz/100 g sugar
2 tablespoons salt
6 juniper berries, crushed
6 whole black peppercorns
1 cinnamon stick
3 whole cloves
2 cloves garlic, bruised
2 bay leaves
1 teaspoon coriander seeds
¹/2 teaspoon fennel seeds

For the vegetables
2 onions, cut in wedges
2 carrots, peeled and cut into strips
10 oz/300 g cauliflower florets
7 oz/200 g stringless green beans, topped, tailed, and halved
1 each red, green, and yellow capsicums (bell peppers),
    seeded and cut into 5–6 segments
2 Lebanese cucumbers, cut into finger lengths, seeds removed
3 green squash, quartered
3 yellow squash, quartered

good-quality olive oil to cover

Place all ingredients for the pickling solution together into a large stainless steel or enamel pan and bring to a boil. Stir to ensure salt and sugar have dissolved.

Add vegetables: first onions then carrots, cauliflower and beans, capsicums, cucumber and squash. Simmer 10–15 minutes in total—the vegetables should remain crunchy.

Drain and spread on paper towels to dry. Pack vegetables into clean sterile jars and fill with oil. Tap bottoms of jars on bench to remove air bubbles. Seal. Check next day to see if oil needs topping up. Can be eaten in 2–3 days. Refrigerate after opening.

fresh lemonade

Fresh lemonade

This refreshing drink can be carried to the picnic in an insulated container.

6 lemons
5 oz/150 g superfine (caster) sugar or to taste
8 cups (64 fl oz/2 l) boiling water
fresh lemon verbena leaves, optional

Scrub lemons well. Using a vegetable peeler, thinly pare the lemons and put the peel into a large bowl. Make sure no pith is attached as it will make the lemonade taste bitter. Add sugar and pour the boiling water over. Stir well to dissolve sugar, then let cool.

Squeeze the juice from the lemons and add to the cooled syrup. Taste and adjust sugar if desired. Refrigerate overnight.

Strain into a jug. Bruise lemon verbena leaves with a wooden spoon and a pinch of sugar to release the essential oils. Add to the jug.

Fresh peaches with mascarpone

This is a luxurious addition to the picnic hamper. Slice fresh peaches into segments. Pile mascarpone into a mound and surround with peach segments. Dip segments into the mascarpone and eat immediately.

Apricot and ricotta tart

If you don't have a food processor, follow the method for making pastry outlined in the recipe for mince pies on page 186.

For the pastry
8 oz/250 g plain (all-purpose) flour
1¹/2 oz/45 g caster (superfine) sugar
¹/2 teaspoon salt
6 oz/185 g cold unsalted butter, roughly chopped
1 large egg
1 tablespoon dry sherry

For the filling
14 oz/400 g dried apricots
piece of orange peel
1 cinnamon stick
4 oz/125 g sugar
2 egg yolks
5 oz/150 g caster (superfine) sugar
zest of 1/2 lemon, finely grated
zest of 1/2 orange, finely grated
1¹/2 lb/750 g fresh ricotta, drained

*P*rocess flour, sugar, and salt in a food processor for a few seconds to combine. Add butter and process until mixture forms breadcrumbs. Add egg and sherry, and process further until combined. Place mixture on a bench and form into a ball. Wrap in waxed (greaseproof) paper and refrigerate for 1 hour.

Preheat oven to 400°F (200°C/Gas 6). Roll out pastry to line a 12 x 8 in (30 x 20 cm) shallow pie pan. Prick pastry lightly with a fork. Return to fridge for 15–20 minutes to allow pastry to relax. Bake the pastry blind—lined with baking paper (parchment) weighed down with dried beans—for 10 minutes. Remove from oven, carefully lift off the paper and beans, and return to oven until pastry is pale gold, about 4–5 minutes. Remove and let stand. Turn oven down to 350°F (180°C/Gas 4).

Place apricots in a saucepan and barely cover with water. Add orange peel, cinnamon stick, and sugar. Bring to a boil and simmer for 20 minutes. Remove from heat and drain.

In a mixing bowl, beat egg yolks with sugar until creamy, then add citrus zest. Beat the ricotta with a fork until light, then add to the egg mixture, and beat until smooth. Pour the ricotta mixture into the prepared pie shell and spread out evenly. Cover with the drained apricots and bake for 40–50 minutes.

Serve cold.

fresh peaches with mascarpone and apricot and ricotta tart

A winter lunch in the kitchen

A winter lunch in the kitchen

Serves 8

Baked Ricotta with Roasted Tomatoes

~

Bollito Misto
served with Vegetables, Salsa Verde,
Mustard, and Horseradish

~

Pannacotta with Poached Apricots

~

Coffee and Tea

Panforte

Savoiardi

*a*n invitation to dine in a friend's kitchen comes straight from the heart. It is a gesture of intimacy, accorded to good friends and members of one's family.

In extending such an invitation, you are inviting people to see who you really are and how you really live, because no matter how well organized, you are bound to slip up (if only a little) at one stage of the proceedings. When you entertain in your dining room—or even outside, for a barbecue—your guests are shielded from the minor dramas that occur in any kitchen.

And that's at least part of the point—entertaining in the kitchen breaks the ice and relieves you of the feeling that everything has to be perfect. You don't have to perform in the way you do for a formal dinner; you can relax a little, take off the mask. In Italy, friends and family actually expect to help in the preparations—it's part of the fun.

On the other hand, a kitchen really is not the place to invite an important business colleague or those you are trying to impress, although it has become so fashionable in some milieus to entertain in this manner that you might just get away with it. A number of leading international hotels now invite certain guests to dine "in the kitchen" with their executive chef or

with a visiting celebrity chef. Such invitations are much sought after, because you, as the guest, are offered a rare glimpse of the inside workings of these vast, gleaming, and hugely impressive kitchens.

The kitchen is the central hub of most homes, used not just for the preparation and cooking of food, but for entertaining and socializing as well. Yet in days gone by, kitchens were built at a distance from the central rooms of the house, sometimes even outdoors. The smell of food was thought to be off-putting and there was the threat of fire. Servants and working-class people actually ate in the kitchen, often sitting around a large wooden table near the fire. It was on this fire, originally, that all meals were cooked. In The Rituals of Dinner, *Margaret Visser* points out that the Latin for hearth or fireplace is "focus", so that where the fire in the house is kept, there is the household's focus. These days, the only time we cook over an open fire is to toast marshmallows or bread, or maybe to roast chestnuts. We've lost that intimate connection with the warm, glowing embers now that we cook in electric or gas ovens. As well, most modern houses are designed with fireplaces (if they have them) in the living areas and not in the kitchen.

If you're fortunate enough to have a fireplace or hearth in your kitchen, use it to advantage. Your guests will feel well-received, for there is something warming and special about eating around a fire with friends. Depending on how confident you feel, you may wish to invite guests in for a drink while you're still preparing the food. Some people are fascinated by the goings-on in a kitchen (the chopping, slicing, blending, stirring, and tasting) and are easily entertained in this way; others are seduced by the delicious smells and aromas of food being cooked.

Choosing a menu

Just as it's become chic to eat in the kitchen, so too has it become the fashion to serve good home cooking. Food that is cooked with love is greatly appreciated, especially in these days of fast foods and store-bought meals. Home-cooked food is very comforting. Most of us carry memories from childhood of time spent in the kitchen with our mothers or grandmothers, and in our adult lives, we are often nostalgic about such experiences.

To take time to put together a well-balanced meal in terms of taste, texture and appearance; to shop for the ingredients and cook them with care are all ways of cherishing your friends. The food doesn't have to be fashionable. A big roast of beef or lamb, served with roasted vegetables, a green vegetable, and a jug of piping hot gravy is always welcome. If you follow this with an apple crumble or baked stuffed apples and some lovely thick cream, your lunch or dinner will be a great success. A hefty pot of thick minestrone served with home-made pesto and crusty bread is perfect for vegetarian guests, followed by a cheese platter and fresh fruit.

For this menu, designed for a winter lunch, the basis is the splendid, wholesome dish from northern Italy called bollito misto or mixed boiled meats. A grand version is served at Christmas or on other festive occasions, although some restaurants in Lombardy and Piedmont still include it on their daily menu. Closely related to the French pot-au-feu, this is a relatively simple meal to prepare for a number of guests. It stretches easily, depending on how many pieces of meat or poultry you add to the pot.

Try to find a pot big enough to hold all the ingredients simultaneously because each lends its taste to the other. The cotechino or Italian sausage, however, is cooked separately as it tends to overpower everything else in the pot. You will need to put the pot on to boil first thing in the morning, as it will take at least 4 hours for the various meats and vegetables to be ready. The meat is put into already boiling stock, the process sealing in the meat's own tasty juices. The flesh should be meltingly tender, but still keep its shape when taken from the pot.

In Italy, guancia (the cheek of the calf's head), calf's foot,

and sometimes the calf's tail are added. The latter two are gelatinous and not to everyone's taste. A piece of boned shoulder of veal is also frequently included. Try to find a good Italian supplier to provide you with the sausage and different cuts. Ask for sausage that is pre-cooked, otherwise it will need considerably longer cooking time. The dish is good served with cannellini beans, which can be bought canned and then warmed gently in another saucepan.

Usually, the whole pot is taken to the table, and the meats pulled out one piece at a time, carved, then returned to the broth until needed. This is less elegant, but it keeps the meats succulent and juicy.

Purchase all the ingredients for this lunch the day before. A good Italian supplier will be able to provide you with delicious savoiardi (sponge fingers) and panforte (fruit and nut cake from Siena), which can be served to your guests with coffee. You can prepare the pannacotta and apricots as well as the first course of baked ricotta and roasted tomatoes then too— serve the ricotta at room temperature and warm the tomatoes before serving. The vegetables for the bollito misto can be prepared first thing in the morning and kept in separate bowls covered with water.

Your guests' interest can be captured by your table as much as your food. An intriguing table is a good talking point. In this case, a variety of gourds have been laid down the middle of the table with the glasses, salt and pepper, the salsa verde, and jugs of water placed amongst them. The folded napkins have been laid across the main plate and a bread roll placed on each.

Wine suggestions

~ With the bollito misto: a savory, mellow Italian red, such as Chianti Classico, or a Barbera from Asti or Alba.

~ With the pannacotta: a sweet wine of individuality, such as Vin Santo from Tuscany, picolit from Friuli, or Jurançon from France.

Baked ricotta with roasted tomatoes

The egg whites make this a lovely, light first course.

2 lb/1 kg ricotta
4 egg whites
melted butter for pan
2 fl oz/60 ml olive oil
1½ teaspoons dried oregano
1 teaspoon dried parsley flakes

For the topping
4 plum (egg) tomatoes, cut in halves lengthwise
1 tablespoon olive oil
1 tablespoon chopped fresh oregano
1 teaspoon flaky sea salt
freshly ground black pepper
black olives, to garnish
extra virgin olive oil, to garnish

Put ricotta into a colander, set in a bowl and cover with plastic wrap. Let drain 2–3 hours in refrigerator. Preheat oven 350°F (180°C/Gas 4).

Beat ricotta and egg whites in a bowl until smooth and well combined. Spoon into a baking dish about 8 x 11 in (20 x 28 cm) that has been lightly brushed with butter. Pour oil over ricotta and distribute evenly with a brush. Sprinkle top with herbs. Bake 30–40 minutes. Set aside and keep at room temperature.

Place tomatoes in a small baking dish with olive oil. Sprinkle with oregano, salt, and pepper, and cook in oven for 15–20 minutes.

Before serving, cut ricotta into squares. Serve garnished with roasted tomatoes and a few black olives. Drizzle with a little more olive oil and any pan juices.

baked ricotta with roasted tomatoes

Bollito misto

The dish is served with salsa verde (see recipe below), mustard, and horseradish.

2 onions, peeled and studded with 2 whole cloves
2 carrots, peeled
3 celery stalks, with their leaves
a few parsley sprigs
1 bay leaf
6–8 black peppercorns
1 fresh beef tongue, 2–3 lb/1–1.5 kg, optional
1 beef shank (shin of beef), bone-in, 2–3 lb/1–1.5 kg
3 teaspoons salt
1 chicken, about 2½ lb/1.25 kg
8 potatoes, scrubbed
8 carrots, peeled
1 pre-cooked cotechino (Italian sausage)
1 cabbage (preferably Savoy), cut into eighths

Place onions, carrots, celery, parsley, bay leaf, and peppercorns into a large pan. Half-fill pan with water and bring to a boil. Add tongue and beef, and bring back to a boil, making sure they are covered with water. Reduce heat to a simmer, and cook for 2–2½ hours, skimming any scum from the surface as it rises.

Remove beef and tongue from the pan. Peel the skin off the tongue. This is best done whilst the tongue is hot—you may want to wear gloves. Slit the skin around the tip of the tongue with a sharp knife and peel it back with your fingers. Trim away any fat and gristle from the root of the tongue. Keep warm under foil.

Add salt and chicken to pan. Let it simmer, for another 45 minutes. Return tongue and beef to pan, and add potatoes and carrots. Bring water back to a boil then simmer until vegetables and chicken are cooked, about 20–30 minutes.

Meanwhile, put the cotechino into a saucepan, cover with water, and bring to a boil. Let simmer 20–30 minutes or until heated through.

Test meats to make sure they are cooked by inserting the point of a sharp knife into the fleshiest part of each. If it pierces through easily, it is done. Using a pair of tongs and a slotted spoon, remove the tongue, beef, chicken, and vegetables from the pan.

Whilst you prepare these, let the cabbage cook in the broth. It will need about 8–10 minutes—be careful not to overcook.

Slice tongue diagonally and arrange on a serving platter. Cut chicken into serving pieces. Remove cotechino from its water, slice it, and add to the platter. You can leave the beef whole if desired, and carve it at the table. Arrange meats on a large platter with vegetables (or use two platters, if desired).

Salsa verde

This vibrant green sauce should be thick and sharp.

1 large bunch watercress, about 1 lb/500 g, stalks removed
4 tablespoons chopped flat-leaf (Italian/continental) parsley
1 small onion, chopped
1 clove garlic, crushed
1 tablespoon lemon juice
5 fl oz/150 ml virgin olive oil
4 anchovy fillets
2 tablespoons capers, drained and chopped
2 gherkins, finely chopped
salt and freshly ground black pepper

Blanch watercress leaves quickly in rapidly boiling salted water. Drain and refresh immediately under cold water. Drain well. Process until smooth in a food processor or blender with parsley, onion, garlic, and lemon juice. Add oil very slowly, blending continually so that sauce does not separate. Add anchovies and blend a further minute or until smooth. Place in a bowl and stir through capers and gherkins. Season to taste, adjusting sharpness—add more lemon juice, salt, pepper, if desired.

Pannacotta

Pannacotta means literally "cooked cream". In this version it is lined with caramel.

12 fl oz/375 ml thickened or whipping cream
3 oz/90 g caster (superfine) sugar
1 piece orange peel
1 piece lemon peel
1 vanilla bean, split in half lengthwise
1 sachet (1/3 oz/10 g) gelatin
4 fl oz/125 ml hot milk
2 fl oz/60 ml Grand Marnier or other orange liqueur
13 fl oz/400 ml light (single) cream
1 tablespoon sugar

For the caramel
4 oz/125 g sugar
2 fl oz/60 ml water

For the apricots
1 lb/500 g fleshy dried apricots
16 fl oz/500 ml water
5 oz/150 g sugar
cinnamon stick
piece orange peel

Place thickened cream, caster sugar, peel, and entire vanilla bean into saucepan. Bring to a boil, stirring to dissolve sugar. Remove from heat, take out peel and bean.

In a bowl mix gelatin and milk. Pour hot cream mixture over gelatin, stirring constantly. Let cool, then stir in Grand Marnier.

Whisk other cream and sugar. When cream forms firm peaks, fold through the cooled cream–gelatin mixture.

Make the caramel by placing sugar and water in a saucepan. Bring to a boil, stirring to dissolve sugar, then let simmer until mixture darkens. Lightly coat the bottoms of eight 7-fl oz (200-ml) dariole molds with the caramel. Spoon cream mixture into the molds. Chill well.

Place all ingredients for the apricots together into a saucepan and bring to a boil, stirring to dissolve sugar. Let simmer gently until apricots are tender but not mushy. Remove from heat and leave to stand in their syrup until ready to serve.

To serve, dip the molds quickly into hot water, then invert each one onto a plate, where the caramel will run out around it. (If it doesn't release immediately, give the plate a strong bang on the bench, holding the mold tightly.) Serve with a few of the poached apricots to one side.

pannacotta

The delights of afternoon tea

The delights of afternoon tea

Serves 16-20 generously

Lemon Sponge Cake

Buttermilk scones
with Strawberry Spoon Jam and Cream

Madeleines

Powidl Tricornes

Nana Phylis' Harvo Loaf

Blueberry Shortcake

Brandy Snaps with Fresh Berries

Sandwiches
Potted Ham ~ Cucumber ~ Rose Petal

Fruit Fools
Raspberry ~ Kiwifruit

Assorted Teas

*i*remember the first time my daughter Natali, then aged four, was invited to afternoon tea. She was filled with anticipation, because it meant seeing her best friend, and she ran around the house in high spirits for most of the day.

That invitation set me thinking. With two young children, it was often difficult to entertain friends—afternoon tea seemed to provide a perfect solution. Most of the food could be prepared well ahead of time, and the children could participate with their own tea party set up separately from the grown-ups. I—to a large extent—could relax and pour tea, a soothing pastime for jaded nerves. And best of all for a tired and busy host, guests departed at a sensible hour.

Since then, this old-fashioned, English custom has become an important way of entertaining for my family. In summer, as we sip our tea, we watch the fall of dusk and the unfolding of fragrant white moonflowers; in winter, we settle around a cosy fire while the children play in the bedrooms.

Afternoon tea is a civil and gentle way to entertain. It is an excellent way to span generations, as both adults and children can enjoy it together. For young children, it is a good introduction to the social graces and subtleties of the table, to the art of considering other people.

At her first afternoon tea party, my daughter helped pour milk into the tea (which was safely lukewarm), add the sugar, pass a plate of cakes, wipe her baby brother's mouth with a napkin—and I've never heard (before or since) so many "pleases", "thank you's" and "excuse me's". Their tea set was made of plastic and their little table covered with a plastic cloth. A "pretend" tea party, in other words, but one at which they could learn some of the rituals associated with afternoon tea.

The old-worldiness of these rituals, combined with mouthwatering edibles and soothing cups of tea, makes the custom of afternoon tea one that most adults view with nostalgia and indulge in with much delight—and appetite.

Choosing the food

An afternoon tea can be as elaborate as you wish. For very young children, the more basic the better, as food is bound to be squashed and drinks spilled. For adults, the offerings may be as simple and heavenly as warm, feathery scones laden with home-made jam, clotted cream, and cups of scalding tea; or as elaborate as a full, formal tea with sandwiches, boiled eggs, buttered toast and crumpets, potted meats, and a variety of cakes, biscuits, and tarts. For hungry appetites, you can add slivers of smoked turkey or chicken breast served on black bread with mild mango chutney, and add a fruit cake to the spread.

"From five o'clock to eight is on certain occasions a little eternity;
but on such an occasion as this the interval could be only an eternity of pleasure."

Henry James, *Portrait of A Lady*

Creating the mood

Whichever mode you choose, keep it as elegant and gracious as possible. On a sunny day, use a balcony or the garden if possible (you can empty the tea leaves straight onto the plants). Spread the table with a pretty cloth. If possible, use two tables, one for the tea and tea implements, the other for the food. Bring out the silver, the cake slicers, linen, and

napkins. Make informal posies of summer flowers and fill bowls with full-blown roses.

Crowd the food table with glass stands adorned with cakes, platters, plates, bowls of fresh summer fruits and other food of your choice. Afternoon tea is an opportunity to indulge in all those wicked concoctions you don't normally eat. Provide sandwich plates and forks. Load the tea table with teapots, cups, saucers (don't worry if they don't all match, as it makes for a lovely jumble), different types of sugars, honey, lemon wedges, and a jug of milk (it was the French, apparently, who added milk and cream to the afternoon tea table). And don't forget the teaspoons.

In winter, set your tables up in front of a large, glowing fire. Use red velvet or velveteen as tablecoths if you can for it will lend a feeling of sumptuousness. Pick flowers in season and pile bowls with oranges. Have a pot of water with a tablespoon or two of ground cinammon simmering on the table before guests arrive to fill the house with a wonderful warm aroma. Make hot chocolate as well as tea. Set up another table for games. Teatime is treat time, so make the setting fanciful and fun.

Finally, to set the mood inside or out, turn on Vivaldi or Handel and let the music dance in the background. A palm court quartet, of course, would fit in very nicely!

Lemon sponge cake

Serve with fresh berries and/or whipped cream, or simply dust with icing (powdered) sugar before serving.

10 oz/300 g caster (superfine) sugar
5 60-g (large)eggs, separated
2 tablespoons lemon juice
water
7 oz/200 g plain (all-purpose) flour
1/2 teaspoon baking powder
3/4 teaspoon cream of tartar
finely grated zest of 1 lemon

*P*reheat oven to 350°F (180°C/Gas 4). Set aside 2 tablespoons of the sugar. Add remaining sugar to egg yolks. Place lemon juice in a measuring cup, and make up to 1/2 cup (4 oz/125 ml) with water. Whisk all together until thickened and sugar is dissolved. Sift flour with baking powder and fold into yolks. Whisk the whites with reserved sugar and cream of tartar until firm. Fold whites and grated zest into yolk–flour mixture.

Pour batter into ungreased 9-in (23-cm) tube or angel food pan. Bake for 50–60 minutes until lightly browned. Remove from oven and turn upside down. Leave until completely cold before releasing from pan.

Buttermilk scones

Makes about 15 scones

Serve with strawberry spoon jam (see recipe opposite) and cream.

1 lb/500 g plain (all-purpose) flour
2 teaspoons bicarbonate of soda (baking soda)
2 teaspoons cream of tartar
2 teaspoons caster (superfine) sugar
1 teaspoon salt
2 oz/60 g unsalted butter, softened
12 fl oz/350 ml buttermilk
milk, for brushing tops

*P*reheat oven to 425°F (220°C/Gas 7). Lightly grease and flour a baking tray.

Sift together the dry ingredients into a mixing bowl. Rub through butter until mixture resembles breadcrumbs. Stir in buttermilk and mix well to combine.

Quickly roll out to 1 in (2.5 cm) thickness and cut into rounds with a 2-in (5-cm) cutter or a small glass dipped in flour. Brush tops lightly with milk. Place the scones side by side on the tray. Bake for 12–15 minutes, until golden. Cool on a wire rack.

Strawberry spoon jam

Makes about 24 fl oz/750 ml

Use tiny wild strawberries if you are lucky enough to have them growing in your backyard. Otherwise, choose the smallest strawberries available. If you cannot locate Jamsetta, use commercial pectin and follow instructions on the packet.

2 lb/1 kg strawberries, hulled and washed
2 fl oz/60 ml lemon juice
1 oz/25 g Jamsetta
1 1/2 lb/750 g sugar

*P*lace strawberries in a saucepan or preserving pan, discarding any that may be bruised. Add lemon juice, and simmer, stirring frequently, until fruit is soft, about 10 minutes. Add Jamsetta and let boil for 1 minute.

Meanwhile, warm sugar in a moderate oven for about 8–10 minutes. Add to the soft fruit and stir until dissolved. Boil quickly for 15–20 minutes. To test for setting, place a saucer into the freezer until cold, then spoon on a little of the jam: if it wrinkles, the jam is set. Leave jam in pan for 10 minutes before pouring into sterile jars. Cover and seal when cold.

Madeleines

Makes about 25 madeleines

4 eggs
4 oz/125 g caster (superfine) sugar
1 teaspoon vanilla essence/extract
4 oz/125 g plain (all-purpose) flour
1 teaspoon baking powder
4 oz/125 g unsalted butter, melted and cooled slightly

*W*hisk eggs, sugar, and vanilla essence until thick and creamy. This will take about 5–7 minutes with an electric beater; the mixture should hold a ribbon trail over the top when you lift the whisk. Sift together flour and baking powder, and fold by hand with a spatula in thirds into the mixture. Add butter with the last third, then refrigerate the bowl for about 20 minutes until the butter hardens slightly.

Meanwhile, preheat oven to 400°F (200°C/Gas 6), and lightly grease and flour madeleine pans.

Spoon in batter until molds are two-thirds full. Bake 10–12 minutes until they have peaked in the middle and are golden brown. Remove from molds and let cool on a cake rack.

lemon sponge cake

Powidl tricorns

A tricorn is a three-cornered hat, in the style for which Napolean was famous. If you cannot find powidl, use a good thick plum jam.

For the pastry
5 oz/150 g unsalted butter, softened
3¹/₂ oz/100 g caster (superfine) sugar
1 egg
8 oz/250 g plain (all-purpose) flour
¹/₂ teaspoon baking powder

For the filling
1 jar powidl (plum purée), about 1 lb/500 g

icing (powdered) sugar

Cream butter and sugar until light and fluffy. Add egg, and cream well. Sift flour with baking powder and stir into creamed butter. Gather mixture into a ball, place on floured board. Cut dough into four wedges. Put one on top of the other and with the heel of your hand, flatten the dough. Repeat twice. Wrap in plastic and refrigerate for 1 hour.

Preheat oven to 375°F (190°C/Gas 5). Roll out onto a floured board to a thickness of about ¹/₄ in (5 mm), being careful not to make it too thin. Cut with a 3-in (7.5-cm) round cutter. Place a tablespoonful of powidl on each circle, gather, and shape into a tricorn. Place on a greased baking sheet. Bake for about 20 minutes or until lightly golden around the edges. Cool on a rack.

Dust with icing sugar before serving.

powidl tricorns

Nana Phylis' Harvo loaf

Make this simple tea bread a day or two ahead so that it has time to mellow. Serve it sliced and buttered.

12 oz/375 g self-raising flour
1/4 teaspoon bicarbonate of soda (baking soda)
8 oz/250 g mixed dried fruit
3 oz/90 g caster (superfine) sugar
8 fl oz/250 ml milk
2 tablespoons golden syrup

Preheat oven to 350°F (180°C/Gas 4). Sift flour and bicarbonate of soda into a mixing bowl. Add dried fruit and sugar, and mix well to combine. Gently heat milk and syrup just long enough to melt syrup. Pour onto dry ingredients and stir until mixture is well combined and stiff in consistency.

Empty into greased 1-lb/500-g loaf pan, and bake for 1 hour. Cool on a cake rack.

Blueberry shortcake

For the pastry
8 oz/250 g cold butter, roughly chopped
1 lb/500 g plain (all-purpose) flour
1 teaspoon baking powder
2 oz/60 g caster (superfine) sugar
finely grated zest of 1/2 lemon
1/2 teaspoon vanilla essence/extract
few drops almond essence/extract
2 tablespoons vegetable oil
1 large egg
1 tablespoon lemon juice

For the filling
14 oz/400 g blueberries, washed and dried
2 oz/60 g caster (superfine) sugar
finely grated zest of 1/2 orange
1/2 teaspoon cinnamon

icing (powdered) sugar, for top

Process butter, flour, baking powder, and caster sugar in a food processor until mixture is crumbly. Add remaining pastry ingredients and process until well combined. Empty onto bench-top and knead into a ball. Wrap in waxed (greaseproof) paper and refrigerate until dough is firm.

Preheat oven to 300°F (150°C/Gas 2).

madeleines, blueberry shortcake

Divide pastry into two, and grate half on the coarse side of a lightly greased 9-in (23-cm) springform pan, covering the bottom completely. Smother with blueberries, and sprinkle with sugar, grated zest, and cinnamon. Grate over the remaining half of pastry, and bake for 1 1/4 hours. Leave in pan until cold. Remove carefully from pan, and dust generously with icing sugar.

Brandy snaps

You may need to experiment with the first batch of these to get them right. Once you've mastered the technique, they're fun to make. It is best to wait until just before serving to fill the snaps with cream, as they soften quickly. Serve with fresh berries.

4 oz/125 g golden syrup
4 oz/125 g unsalted butter
4 oz/125 g brown sugar
4¹/2 oz/135 g plain (all-purpose) flour
3 teaspoons ground ginger

For the filling
10 fl oz/300 ml cream
2 teaspoons brandy, or to taste
2 tablespoons icing (powdered) sugar

Preheat oven to 400°F (200°C/Gas 6). Lightly grease a large baking sheet.

Place golden syrup, butter, and sugar into a saucepan, and heat gently until melted. Remove from heat. Sift together flour and ginger, and stir into the butter mixture. Drop 4–5 teaspoonfuls on to the baking tray, allowing plenty of room for spreading. (It is best to cook only a few biscuits at a time so that you can work with them as they cool). Bake for 5 minutes or until bubbly and golden.

Remove from oven and, as the mixture begins to firm, roll each one quickly around the handle of a wooden spoon or lightly greased cornet mold. Work quickly, as the snaps harden as they cool. Leave until set. Let cool on a wire rack.

Whip cream with brandy and icing sugar, and pipe into rolled snaps.

Ribbon sandwiches

Use either brown or white pre-sliced bread, depending on your preference. Allow one sandwich (or three "fingers") per person. Each sandwich will require three slices of bread, and there are usually about 21 slices in each loaf, or enough for seven people. Alternate white with brown bread to give a pretty checkerboard effect.

Allow about 8 oz/250 g softened or creamed butter for each loaf of bread. Make sure it is at room temperature so that it is easy to spread (right to the edges). If you beat it, it will be lighter and easier to work with. Use a palette knife to spread. Remove the crusts with a serrated knife once you have filled and topped the sandwich.

Keep the sandwiches fresh by covering with a clean damp cloth and refrigerating until ready to use. Alternatively, use a piece of wetted waxed (greaseproof) paper which has been wrung out, then cover tightly with plastic wrap.

brandy snaps

Potted ham sandwiches

Makes about 12 oz/375 g, enough for 18–21 fingers

Make sure this is at room temperature before spreading.

8 oz/250 g smoked ham, skin removed
4 oz/125 g unsalted butter, softened
2–3 teaspoons dry mustard
pinch cayenne pepper
pinch nutmeg
salt
2¹/2 oz/75 g clarified butter, melted
18-21 slices pre-sliced white and brown bread
4 oz/125 g unsalted butter, softened and lightly whipped
watercress leaves, optional

Dice ham, making sure you include a little of its fat. Process in a food processor with butter, mustard, cayenne, and nutmeg until finely puréed. Season with salt to taste. Empty into a pot or ramekin dish and spoon over clarified butter to form a thin film. Refrigerate until ready to use.

When making sandwiches, spread bread lightly with butter. For each sandwich, layer 3 slices together, the lower 2 each spread with a good tablespoonful of the potted ham; a few watercress leaves are a welcome addition. Trim crusts, and cut sandwiches into three equal "fingers" or "ribbons".

Cucumber sandwiches

Makes about 15 fingers

2 Lebanese or continental cucumbers, about 6-in (15-cm)
*   long, or 1 telegraph cucumber, about 12 in (30 cm),*
*   very finely sliced*
salt
1 teaspoon virgin olive oil
white pepper, optional
15 slices pre-sliced white and brown bread
6 oz/185 g unsalted butter, softened and lightly whipped

Place cucumber slices in a non-corrosive colander. Sprinkle lightly with salt, toss, and set aside to drain for 1 hour.

Press down the slices with a plate or the palm of your hand to remove any excess juices. Dress cucumber slices with oil and pepper.

Spread bread with butter. For each sandwich, layer 3 slices together, the lower 2 topped with cucumber slices. Trim crusts and cut into 3 equal "fingers" or "ribbons."

Rose petal sandwiches

Makes about 9 fingers

Make sure you use petals which have not been sprayed with pesticide, and that you remove the white triangular heel from the base. Choose fragrant roses in season. Allow 2 medium roses for each sandwich.

4 oz/125 g unsalted butter, softened
a few drops of rosewater
1–2 teaspoons icing (powdered) sugar, or to taste
9 slices pre-sliced white bread
6 medium roses, washed and dried

ribbon sandwiches

*L*ightly whip butter with rosewater and confectioners' sugar.

For each sandwich, spread 3 slices of bread with butter. Stack slices together, trim crusts, and cut into 3 even fingers. Fill the 2 layers of each finger with petals, letting them overflow the edges slightly so that the petals show. Decorate the plate with extra rose petals.

A modern "conceit" to serve at your afternoon tea. In his book, Afternoon Tea, *Michael Smith describes the English eighteenth-century custom of indulging in "subtleties" and "conceits" like rich creams and exotic jellies. These were served after a morning in the pleasure gardens or Assembly Rooms in Bath, and the habit gradually transferred to the afternoon tea table. Ice-creams, jellies, custards, syllabubs, and sack (or sherry) creams were all popular. "Next time you give a tea-party," says Smith, "present a selection of them on silver salvers or glass plates—they will surprise and delight your guests."*

Raspberry fool

Serves 6

1 lb/500 g raspberries
4 oz/110 g caster (superfine) sugar
1 teaspoon lemon juice, or to taste
10 fl oz/300 ml cream
1 egg white, optional

*B*lend raspberries and sugar in a blender until puréed. Press through a sieve into a bowl. Add lemon juice to taste. Whip cream and egg white until thick and light, then fold into fruit purée. Spoon into individual serving glasses and chill well.

Kiwi fruit fool

Serves 6

6 kiwi fruit, peeled and roughly chopped
10 fl oz/300 ml cream
1 egg white
4 oz/110 g caster (superfine) sugar

*P*urée kiwi fruit flesh in a blender, then press through a sieve to remove black seeds (although some black seeds look rather pretty flecked through the cream). Whip cream with egg white and sugar until thick and light, then fold into fruit purée. Spoon into individual serving glasses and chill well.

Strawberry leaf tea

"Gather the leaves while young and tender, pick off the stalks, and dry in an airy, but shady place. When a sufficient quantity is collected, and the whole is perfectly dry, it may be kept in a canister or bottle, as other teas, and used in the same manner."

Anne Scott James, *The Cottage Garden* (1840)

Making tea

Tea is a great restorative so it is worth learning the art of making a good pot.

Choose a variety of interesting teas. Darjeeling and English Breakfast are good standbys and fragrant teas such as rose petal and Earl Grey are also appealing. If you want to be more adventurous, you could brew a pot of chai, the delicious spiced milky tea that is so popular in India. Try teas made with strawberry leaves or add a few rose leaves to a pot of ordinary black tea. Offer herbal teas such as chamomile and peppermint, or if you grow fresh herbs, experiment with those.

Tea bags are definitely out. Although convenient, they in no way equate with the full-bodiedness of properly brewed tea, and they detract from the elegance of the occasion.

Pay attention to the finer details and you will taste the difference.

~ Use freshly boiled water but do not over-boil it. Water that is kept boiling tends to become de-aerated.

~ Heat the teapot beforehand by rinsing with boiling water.

~ Allow one teaspoon of tea leaves per cup of water to be used, plus one teaspoon more "for the pot". Add more hot water once the tea has brewed if you prefer it weaker.

~ Pour on the boiling water, cover and set aside for 3 minutes.

~ Lift cover, stir, and strain into tea cups.

~ Serve black or with lemon and honey, or with milk, or milk and sugar.

To prevent tea from "stewing", you could follow Mrs Beeton's advice and make the tea in one pot, let it infuse for 5 minutes, then decant through a tea-strainer into a second, warmed teapot.

For herbal teas, experiment with quantity per cup. As a general guideline, allow $1/2$-1 tablespoon of fresh herbs, or $1/4$-$1/2$ teaspoon of dried per cup. For mild herbs, double this amount. Sweeten with honey if desired, but do not add milk or sugar.

An impromptu meal from the pantry

An impromptu meal from the pantry

Serves 6-8

Bresaola with Mixed Leaf Salad and Parmesan

Frittata di Maccheroni Farcita

Spaghetti All'Insalata

Penne All'Aglio e Olio

~

Paula's Meringues

Pears and Cheese

*W*hen you live in the fast lane, planning ahead and being well organized are major survival skills. Often, after a long day of rushing around and working hard, the very thought of preparing dinner can be an anathema. Even more so when your partner or perhaps one of your children calls late in the day to tell you that unexpected guests will be coming for dinner. In the midst of an important business meeting, you can suddenly find yourself panicking. "Have I got anything to cook for dinner tonight? What's in the pantry? Is there anything I can quickly pull out of the freezer?" Yet if your kitchen is cleverly stocked, there's no need for such attacks of anxiety.

Organizing your kitchen

A well-stocked and ordered pantry can give you a great feeling of satisfaction and plenitude. If you do not already have your pantry in order, make it a New Year's (or even mid-year's) resolution to do so. You may be surprised by what you find (if you're a hoarder by nature) or don't find (if you're like Mother Hubbard). Throw out any item that has passed its "use-by" date. Use the suggestions provided in this chapter to work out a master list of staples. Assemble similar items in one section of the pantry: store all sugars, salts, rice, and pastas together; all the canned foods, sweet and savory; all the stocks, herbs, spices, oils and vinegars. Label everything clearly. Any food that sits undisturbed for a month or more, especially during summer, is a potential breeding ground for insects. During hot weather,

items such as flour, bran, wheatgerm, and whole grains should be stored in the refrigerator, as the cold will prevent breeding of worms and moths. Storage containers are important and should be thoughtfully considered. When purchasing, select those made from glass, metal, or heavy plastic, and make sure their lids are secure and tight-fitting.

Don't forget the refrigerator and freezer. These too are invaluable storage places for everything from bread and packaged foods through to pre-prepared home-made quiches, pies, pasta sauces, curries, casseroles, sorbets, crêpes, icecreams, and cakes. As with the pantry, these items should be stored in plastic freezer bags or plastic containers, and clearly labeled, preferably with a record of the date on which they were made.

Perhaps your actual storage area needs to be examined. Pantry design has been rather neglected over the past few decades as the open-plan kitchen emphasized living space rather than storage space. Deep shelves are important to protect delicate items such as oils, nuts, baking powders, and chocolate from light.

Ideas for easy entertaining

Maybe your concept of entertaining needs a rethink. What is your motivation in inviting friends in to your home? To impress, or to give pleasure and enjoy their company? Sometimes we put off inviting people because we feel that if we do so we have to go to a lot of trouble. You don't have to present a formal dinner every time you entertain: a pasta dish, a salad, and a bottle or two of wine are all that is needed to make old friends feel welcome. Mediterranean cuisine is ideal for stylish, approachable dishes that can be easily assembled from ingredients on hand.

You will find that you can achieve maximum effort with minimum fuss if you're organized and if your mind is open to new and different ideas. Consider the lowly lentil, for example. Brown lentils can be made into a delicious soup with staples from the pantry. Soften them first, then throw them into a saucepan with some canned tomatoes, tomato puree, stock, olive oil, and garlic and season with salt, pepper, and ground cumin. Cook for 20 minutes, then give the soup a whirl in the food processor. Served in pristine white soup bowls, this is a sensational and hearty soup. Red lentils too can be spiced in hundreds of different ways and served as dhal with rice, fish, and meat dishes. The spicing is what counts—try ginger, onion, garlic, chili, mustard seeds, ground coriander, and cumin. All these should be staples in your kitchen. Think about growing herbs in your garden or in an indoor container for a constant supply of fresh herbs to add life to any meal.

"Then there are all your sauces, mustards, pickles, chutneys, capers, salad-dressings and oils. Splendid. So those cupboards are for tinned food and you have selected them so that at any time you could feed four people for a week on nothing else? You're a wonder, Mrs Scoop; I wish there were more like you."

Rupert Croft-Cooke, *English Cooking*

so many shapes and sizes, is inexpensive, nutritious, and can be bought fresh, frozen, or dried. Quick to prepare, you can easily make a dish for four or forty-four.

Different-shaped pastas go with different sauces. Spaghetti, spaghettini, and vermicelli are best with olive oil-based sauces that have bulky whole ingredients—such as vegetables or seafood—tossed through them. The long strands wrap around the ingredients with ease. One of the quickest and most delicious preparations, spaghetti all'insalata, is featured on page 95. Penne (which means "quills") comes both smooth and ridged ("rigate") and goes well with almost any sauce. Rigatoni and macaroni are best with dense sauces. Flat pastas such as tagliatelle and fettuccine are good with a meat sauce and when fresh go well with creamy sauces which coat their broad surfaces. Pappardelle, the very wide flat pasta, is excellent with rich sauces made from game

Arborio, or short round-grained rice, can be made into any number of risotto dishes. The addition of fresh or dried vegetables (such as porcini and tomatoes) and a little white wine or even champagne will enliven and change the basic recipe in countless ways. Canned tomatoes are an indispensable item for soups, sauces, and pizza tops; and dried fruits and nuts come in handy for eating just as they are or for use in baking biscuits, cakes, and meringues.

Perhaps the greatest standby of all is pasta. It comes in

and oxtail. Always serve pasta al dente, a term which means "to the tooth"—it should be neither crunchy nor limp. The only way to really know whether it is cooked is to taste it.

When Italians have a feast of pasta they call it a spaghettata—it's a good idea for supper, or for a low-key dinner or lunch, whether planned or unplanned. A good place to entertain unexpected guests is in your kitchen. Set up the table with a fresh tablecloth and napkins, keeping it casual. For a change from flowers, use vegetables as a decorative element (we've used mini ones on our table).

Suggestions for the panic-proof gourmet pantry

artichoke hearts (plain or marinated)

baking powder, bicarbonate of soda, dry yeast

beans and legumes— *cannellini, chick peas, soy*

breadcrumbs

capers

chili—*hot and sweet chili sauce, fresh dried, or minced and bottled*

chocolate—*dark, milk, white*

corn chips (for dips)

crab meat (canned)

crackers

curry paste or powder

dry yeast

fish (canned)—*anchovies, salmon, sardines, tuna in oil*

flour—*white and wholemeal, all-purpose (plain) and self-raising*

fruits (canned)—*apricots, halved peaches, stewed apple*

fruits (dried)—*apples, apricots, currants, dates, figs, prunes, raisins, sultanas*

gelatine

grains—*couscous, oats, polenta, quinoa*

herbs (dried)—*basil, bay leaves, dill, marjoram, oregano, parsley, rosemary, sage, thyme*

honey, golden syrup, maple syrup

lentils—*brown and red*

liqueurs—*brandy, dry sherry, Grand Marnier, rum, white and red wine*

mayonnaise

mushrooms (dried)—*porcini*

mustard—*Dijon, whole-grain*

oils -— *extra virgin olive, virgin olive, olive, sesame, vegetable*

olives and olive paste

pasta—*fettuccine, macaroni, penne, spaghetti*

pepper—*black peppercorns, white pepper*

pesto (buy it in a sealed jar)

rice—*arborio, brown, long-grain white, wild*

salt—*cooking salt, flaky sea salt*

sauces—*fish, ketchup, soy, tahini, Worcestershire*

seeds—*poppy, sesame, sunflower*

spices—*allspice, cayenne pepper, cinnamon, cloves, coriander, cumin, ground ginger, mustard powder and seeds, paprika, saffron, tumeric, vanilla beans or essence*

stocks—*beef, chicken, vegetable*

sugar—*brown, caster (superfine), icing (powdered), white*

tomatoes—*canned plum (egg), paste or purée, sun-dried*

vinegars— *balsamic, champagne, red and white wine*

In a dark, well-ventilated cupboard:

onions of various kinds

oranges and lemons (use the rind and the juice)

potatoes

Suggestions for the panic-proof refrigerator

apples

carrots

cheese—*brie, cheddar, mozzarella, parmesan*

cured, packaged meats—*bacon, salami, smoked salmon or trout*

celery

eggs

fetta cheese (buy it in a sealed jar)

garlic (whole and fresh, or minced and bottled)

ginger (whole and fresh, or minced and bottled)

milk, cream

nuts—*almonds, cashews, hazelnuts, pecans, pine nuts, pistachio, walnuts*

Suggestions for the panic-proof freezer

bread—*French bread sticks, wholegrain loaf*

berries

butter—*salted, unsalted*

icecream and sorbets

pancakes and crêpes

pastry—*ready-rolled filo, puff pastry, shortcrust*

vegetables—*peas*

a home-made cake or two

Ideas for dishes you can create from your pantry

~ Beans, either the canned or dried varieties make good salads. For example, cannellini beans tossed with drained canned tuna, tomato wedges, onion rings, and black olives.

~ Curry pastes take all the work out of curries made with vegetables (the humble potato with frozen peas makes a great curry), or with meat or chicken (from your freezer).

~ Flour can be made into pizza bases, focaccia, and breads with dry yeast, as well as scones, biscuits, and cakes.

~ Pancakes and crêpes can be served with either savory or sweet fillings.

~ Pasta can be served hot tossed with a commercial pesto and a little cream; or with tomato-based sauces, a little basil (fresh or dried), and freshly grated parmesan cheese. Or use it cold mixed with different salad ingredients.

~ Potatoes can be baked whole and filled with bolognese sauce and cheese or sour cream and cheese; or made into a tortilla (a Spanish omelette); or a potato salad dressed with toasted sunflower and sesame seeds.

~ Rice satisfies either as a risotto or, for dessert, as a rice pudding.

~ Soups can be served straight from the can and enhanced with extra fresh vegetables and herbs.

Wine suggestions

~ *With the bresaola:* a fresh, crisp young white wine, such as Vernaccia di San Gimignano, or a Condrieu or Hermitage blanc from the Rhône Valley.

~ *With the pasta dishes:* a full-bodied, rich, fruity Australian or Californian chardonnay or, from Italy, a trebbiano d' Abruzzo or one of the richer Gavi from Piedmont.

Bresaola with mixed leaf salad and parmesan

Bresaola is cured, dried beef from the Lombardy region of Italy; you can buy it at good delicatessens. Or you can use prosciutto or any cold sliced meat.

8 tablespoons virgin olive oil
2 tablespoons red wine vinegar
salt and freshly ground black pepper
11–13 oz (350–400 g) mixed leaves, washed and dried
3¹/₂ oz/100 g parmesan, in one piece
3¹/₂ oz/100 g bresaola, thinly sliced

*P*lace oil, vinegar, salt, and pepper in a small bowl, and beat together with a fork. Pour over mixed leaves and toss lightly to coat. Pile in the middle of a serving platter or on individual plates.

Using a vegetable peeler, shave flakes of parmesan directly onto leaves. Arrange bresaola in overlapping slices around salad. Serve immediately.

Frittata di maccheroni farcita

Serves 6 as a main course, 8 as an appetizer or as one of a number of dishes

melted butter and dry breadcrumbs for pan
1 teaspoon salt
1 lb/500 g tagliarini or vermicelli
2 tablespoons olive oil
1 lb/500 g ripe tomatoes, peeled, seeded, and diced
4 eggs
3 tablespoons freshly grated parmesan
salt and freshly ground black pepper
3¹/₂ oz/100 g salami, diced
2 hard-boiled eggs, sliced
3¹/₂ oz/100 g mozzarella, sliced
2 tablespoons pesto (commerical or home-made)
2 oz/50 g unsalted butter

*P*reheat oven to 350°F (180°C/Gas 4). Grease a 9-in (23-cm) cake pan with deep sides, and sprinkle lightly and evenly with dry breadcrumbs.

Bring a large pan of water to a boil, add salt, then pasta, and cook until al dente. Drain, rinse in cold water, and set aside in a large bowl.

Meanwhile, heat oil in a frying pan. Add tomatoes, and cook for a few minutes until softened but not dry. Season to taste.

In a bowl, whisk eggs. Add parmesan, salt, and pepper. Pour egg mixture over pasta and mix well to combine. Fill the prepared pan with half the pasta. Scatter salami over the top, then egg slices, and mozzarella. Spread with cooked tomatoes and pesto. Cover with remaining pasta and scatter flakes of butter over the top.

Bake for 45 minutes or until top is crusty and nicely browned. Remove from oven. Leave in pan for 5 minutes before turning out onto cooling rack. Place a serving plate on top of frittata and turn over again. Serve warm.

Spaghetti all'insalata

Serves 4 as a main course, 5–6 as an appetizer or more as one of a selection of pastas

This translates from Italian as "spaghetti with salad" and is a specialty of Positano, near Naples.

1 lb/500 g ripe egg (plum) tomatoes
1/2 red onion, finely chopped
2 stalks celery, thinly sliced
1–2 cloves garlic, crushed
1 tablespoon fresh basil, finely chopped
1 tablespoon fresh oregano, finely chopped
1 tablespoon flat-leaf (Italian/continental) parsley,
    finely chopped
3–4 tablespoons virgin olive oil

salt and freshly ground black pepper
1 teaspoon salt
1 lb/500 g spaghetti
salt for water

*P*eel tomatoes by plunging quickly into rapidly boiling water. Transfer to a bowl of cold water and slip off skins. Cut into quarters lengthwise and remove seeds. Put into a large serving bowl with onion, celery, garlic, and herbs. Pour over oil, and season with salt and pepper. Set aside.

Bring a large pan of water to boil. Add salt and spaghetti. Cook until al dente. Drain, and toss immediately through the prepared vegetables. Taste for seasoning. Serve at once.

spaghetti all'insalata

penne all'aglio e olio

Penne all'aglio e olio

This dish of penne with garlic and oil serves 4 as a main course, 5–6 as an appetizer, or more as one of a number of pastas

1 lb/500 g penne rigate
salt
3–4 cloves garlic, slivered
1 small red chili, seeds left in, finely sliced
3¹/2 fl oz/100 ml extra virgin olive oil
3 tablespoons freshly grated parmesan
freshly ground black pepper
extra small red chilis, for garnish
extra parmesan, for serving

Bring a large pan of water to a boil, add salt, and then the penne. Cook until al dente, then drain. Whilst pasta is cooking, place garlic, chili (with its seeds), and oil into a large serving bowl. Toss hot pasta through the oil mixture. Add parmesan and toss again. Season to taste with salt and pepper. Garnish with extra small red chilis. Serve with extra cheese on the side.

Paula's meringues

Makes about 25 sensational meringues

3 egg whites
7 oz/200 g caster (superfine) sugar
7 oz/200 g pitted (stoned) dates, chopped
3¹/2 oz/100 g walnuts, chopped
3¹/2 oz/100 g slivered almonds

Preheat oven to 250°F (120°C/Gas 1/2). Grease and flour a baking sheet.

Place egg whites and sugar in the top of a double-boiler over hot water. Whisk until very thick. Remove from heat and gently fold through dates and nuts. Drop spoonfuls onto prepared baking sheet and bake for 1 hour. Turn off oven and leave meringues to dry in oven for another hour. Store in an airtight container.

Pears and cheese

Finish off the meal with meringues and a platter of pears and cheese. Slice the pears and serve with a wedge of parmesan and some store-bought mascarpone reale (mascarpone mixed with gorgonzola cheese).

pears and cheese

A dinner party

A dinner party

Serves 6

Mini Farm Tarts

Champagne

~

Dressed Mudcrab Salad with Mayonnaise

~

**Spatchcock with Basil Butter
and Mixed Mushrooms**

**Spaghetti Tossed in Butter, Black Pepper,
and Parmesan**

Herb Toast

~

Poached Peaches with Strawberry Puree

Apricot Tart with Home-Made Vanilla Icecream

~

Coffee and Petits Fours

*t*he best time to hold a formal dinner party is when you feel like doing something special. This means in every way—with the food, the composition of the menu, the setting of the table, the flowers, and the ambience you create.

Perhaps you want to see very old friends who mean a lot to you and this is your way of showing them your esteem. Maybe you need to entertain business colleagues in a home environment (a sure way to forge bonds). Or it could be an occasion such as meeting your daughter's future in-laws for the first time.

Whatever the reason, by definition the word "formal" means something required by convention; a precise, regular observation of the rules. An occasion on which you put your best foot forward. This does not mean, however, that your dinner has to be prim and stiff. Gone are the days of overly-

formal dinners—except, I guess, when dining with ministers-of-state or royalty. Elegance and a certain sense of ceremony are called for, but not intimidating grandeur. Nor should this be an occasion for exhibitionism—guests should be invited because you enjoy their company and wish to further a connection with them. On the other hand, it is a pity to have a well set-up dining room and never use it, something which happens rather frequently in these more informal times.

A formal dinner is a lovely thing to do occasionally and gives you a chance to put away your everyday odds and ends, and bring out any splendid items saved for special occasions.

Choosing a menu

Like any occasion, though, where food is involved, it should be enjoyable, not daunting. It doesn't have to be hugely expensive either, or impossibly complicated. If you plan your menu well and according to foods that are in season, you can have a fabulous meal without breaking the bank. In winter, for example, an elegant casserole makes a perfect main course and usually improves if made one or two days ahead. Make a list of dishes you'd like to serve and feel comfortable about cooking. Choose a first course that can be made ahead and which requires little last-minute assembling. Most desserts can also be made well ahead. Cheese? Well, some people do and some don't. If you decide to offer a cheese course, serve it before the dessert unless its the classic nine-course dinner party where the cheese is served eighth (see page 10 for the chapter on etiquette). Balance the cheeses you serve: a creamy one, a blue, a cheddar, and perhaps a goat cheese. Remove from the refrigerator (and their wrappings) 1 or 2 hours before serving.

Guidelines for a successful formal dinner

The major difference between a "formal" and a "casual" dinner party these days is marked by style of dress. When sending invitations to a formal dinner, specify the type of dress you would like the guests to wear. A formal written invitation with "black tie stipulated", rather than a telephone call, will help set the scene.

1. Call, fax or write to invite people three to four weeks ahead. Send out a list of the other guests so that people know who they will be dining with—it must be an enjoyable evening for everyone. Always allow guests the opportunity to decline.

2. Dinner should not be late or too drawn out. Invite people to come at 7 pm for 7.30 pm. Serve the hors d'oeuvres and champagne by 7.15 pm, the first course at 8 pm, and finish closer to 11 pm than midnight. Midweek especially, people may get tired.

3. Keep things moving along—don't let people sit with plates in front of them.

4. Be organized. Have as much prepared ahead as possible with everything chopped and ready. Try to choose dishes that can be cooked almost completely in advance.

5. Keep it simple. Stick to things you can do easily and well—while able to talk at the same time.

6. Keep it tasty, not tricky. Forget the latest trends if they're not for you. Good home cooking is enjoyed by most. Some of my best dinners are those with well-loved, proven winners like fish, fries, salad, and desserts such as rhubarb crumble.

7. Don't overload people. Rich chocolate cake is not for everyone, so if you like it, keep portions small (at first) and offer a light and cleaner alternative (such as a poached peach or pear), as well.

8. It's a good idea to find out in advance the dietary preferences of guests. Many people today prefer vegetable and seafood dishes to red meat.

The number of courses you decide to serve will depend on what you feel comfortable with, the number of guests, the occasion, and how much help you have. These days, three or maybe four courses is usual, five at most.

This menu

The menu suggestions here are achievable yet sophisticated and come from a dinner party held at the home of former chef and restaurateur Jenny Ferguson; the guidelines for a successful dinner are also hers. She has noticed a big shift in the past few years in attitudes towards these functions—more relaxed, more philsophical while still remaining "formal".

Mini farm tarts are served as an hors d'oeuvre with champagne before moving to the table. The toppings can be varied endlessly with different types of cheese (brie, goat's) and vegetables. Halved cherry tomatoes work particularly well. The spatchcock is quick, easy, and tastes heavenly. The pasta should be good enough to eat on its own. Make sure you toss it with lots of black pepper, butter, and cheese. For dessert, why not offer a choice and serve it at the table? To finish, petits fours with coffee. There is no need to expend effort on making these at home—delicious petits fours are widely available at specialty food stores.

mini farm tarts

Preheat oven to 425°F (220°C/Gas 7). Roast eggplant with a small drizzling of olive oil until soft, then chop into small pieces. Roast capsicum then skin by sealing in a plastic bag until the skin steams off. Chop capsicum flesh into small pieces.

Combine leftover pieces of puff pastry, roll out, and cut circles with a small cutter. Place on a greased baking sheet. Spread with tomato sauce. Top each with a piece of eggplant and capsicum. Crumble blue cheese on top and sprinkle with chives and parmesan. Chill in the refrigerator until a few minutes before guests are expected, then bake until puffed and golden, about 8-10 minutes. If timing is tricky, half-cook, and finish as guests arrive.

Dressed mudcrab salad

The dressing for the crabs is a simple vinaigrette. The dish can be served with a bowl of cut lemons and, if you like, another bowl of mayonnaise mixed with chopped capers, sweet gherkins, and chives.

2 live mudcrabs, each about 2 lb/1 kg
6 fl oz/160 ml virgin olive oil
3 fl oz/80 ml balsamic vinegar
1 teaspoon grain mustard
pinch salt
freshly ground black pepper
about 6 handfuls mixed salad leaves (e.g. oak leaf, curly endive, arugola/rocket, chervil), washed and dried
2 ripe avocados, peeled and sliced
6 lemons, cut in quarters

For the mayonnaise
2 egg yolks
1 teaspoon salt
1 teaspoon pepper
1 teaspoon lemon juice
8 fl oz/250 ml olive oil

Mini farm tarts

The quantities for these tarts are not precise, as they are made with tasty odds and ends from the refrigerator, including (perhaps) pastry leftover from the apricot tart in this menu. It is best to use fresh tomato sauce (purée), and Blue Castello works well as the blue cheese. Allow two tarts per person, plus a few extra.

2 medium slices eggplant (aubergine)
1 small red capsicum (bell pepper)
small leftover pieces of puff pastry (commercial or see the recipe on page 111)
blue cheese
few tablespoons tomato sauce (purée)
freshly chopped chives
freshly grated parmesan
olive oil
freshly ground black pepper

dressed mudcrab salad

Choose live crabs, take straight home, and place still wrapped in the freezer for a couple of hours to "put to sleep." Only then plunge them into boiling water. Bring back to a boil and continue cooking for a further 15 minutes. When done, plunge into cold water to cool, then shell. Make sure there are no small bits of shell left clinging to the meat. All this can be done the day before and the crab meat refrigerated until needed.

Make the dressing by whisking together oil, vinegar, mustard, salt, and pepper, until well combined; adjust according to taste.

Toss salad leaves with dressing and lay a pile on each plate. Place a few slices of avocado on the leaves. Divide crab meat into six portions. Gently squeeze to mold each one into a ball (this helps to remove excess moisture and to give the flesh shape) and place on top of avocado. Squeeze lemons over to taste (serve remainder in a bowl), and top with a brisk grinding of pepper.

To make the mayonnaise, place egg yolks, salt, pepper, and lemon juice in a bowl. With a balloon whisk, combine well, and continue to whisk whilst adding oil, a few drops at a time to begin. As mixture begins to thicken, continue to add oil in a steady stream. It should become thick and creamy.

Spatchcock with basil butter and mixed mushrooms

The pasta used in this recipe is freshly-made; if using dried packet spaghetti, the cooking time extends to 7–9 minutes. To serve the dish, spoon hot mushrooms into the middle of hot dinner plates. Arrange spatchcock (a young chicken) portion on top. Serve spaghetti separately in a large bowl so that it can be passed around.

6 fresh free-range spatchcocks (see glossary),
     each 13 oz/400 g
6 oz/185 g softened butter
6 tablespoons chopped fresh basil
salt and freshly ground black pepper
extra butter, for cooking
3 cups mixed fresh mushrooms (e.g. field, button, shiitake,
     Swiss browns, ups), larger ones chopped
1/4 cup (2 fl oz/60 ml) cream

For the spaghetti
1 lb/500 g fresh spaghetti
2 teaspoons butter
2 tablespoons freshly grated parmesan
freshly ground black pepper
extra grated parmesan for serving

T rim off wing tips at the first joint from the body. Starting at the neck, slice down either side of the breastbone, so as to remove the flesh from the carcass in two halves, leaving only the wing and leg bones attached.

Preheat grill (broiler) to hot.

Mix butter and basil together. Lay the bird halves, skin-side down to start, on a flat tray, dot with the basil butter, season with salt and pepper, and cook for 7–8 minutes each side, until they are golden and juices run clear when meat is pierced with a knife or skewer.

Melt more butter in a large hot frying pan and toss mushrooms together with a good pinch salt and a grinding of black pepper. Sauté mushrooms until just softened. Stir in cream. Spoon over spatchcock.

Cook spaghetti at the last moment in rapidly boiling salted water until just tender, about 2 minutes. When cooked, drain well, toss in butter, 2 tablespoons parmesan, and a dusting of pepper. Serve with a separate bowl of parmesan for guests to help themselves.

Herb toast

1 baguette (thick French bread stick), sliced diagonally
butter, softened
chopped herbs (e.g. chives, parsley)

P reheat oven to 350°F (180°C/Gas 4). Mix butter with herbs. Spread herb butter on both sides of bread, arrange in a single layer on a baking tray, and bake in oven until golden and crisp.

Strawberry purée

P urée 1 lb/500 g hulled strawberries with caster (superfine) sugar to taste. Add sugar gradually. Chill. Serve with choice of desserts.

Apricot tart

Serve this tart with a bowl of thick fresh cream, or vanilla icecream (see recipe overleaf).

puff pastry (commercial or see recipe overleaf)
ripe apricots, halved and pitted (stoned)
water
4–8 oz/125–250 g sugar
extra sugar, for sprinkling

For caramel butter
4 oz/110 g caster (superfine) sugar
8 fl oz/250 ml water
2 oz/50 g unsalted butter

R oll out pastry very thinly and cut out a circle to fit a 10 in (24 cm) diameter tart or quiche dish. Chill pastry while you prepare apricots (enough halves to cover dish).

Place apricots into a pan, cover with water and sugar, and poach gently until just tender—don't let them become soft and squishy. Drain and put them rounded side down in the bottom of the unlined tart or quiche dish.

Preheat oven to 375°F (190°C/Gas 5).

Make the caramel butter by cooking sugar and water in a frying pan until a light golden caramel. Add butter. Let this mixture bubble for a couple of minutes, then pour over apricots. Cover with pastry. Sprinkle some extra sugar over and bake for 45–60 minutes, or until pastry is crisp. Trim off excess pastry edges and tip upside down onto a plate.

herb toast, spatchcock with basil butter and mixed mushrooms

"True gourmets always have finished their meal before the sweet.
All that they eat later is by politeness, but gourmets are usually very polite."

Grimod de la Reynière, in *Gambols in Gastronomy* by William Wallace Irwin

vanilla icecream, poached peaches, apricot tart, strawberry purée

Vanilla icecream

You'll need an icecream maker for this recipe. If you don't have one, buy top quality commercial icecream—it makes a difference. Don't throw away the used vanilla beans that feature in this recipe. They can be washed and put into your sugar jar to perfume the sugar, or they can be added to your next icecream, together with fresh beans.

28 fl oz/800 ml cream
2 good vanilla beans
1 teaspoon pure vanilla, optional
8 egg yolks
4¹/₂ oz/125 g caster (superfine) sugar

Pour cream into a saucepan. Split vanilla bean lengthwise and scrape all the powdery black seeds into the cream, as well as the scraped pods. Add pure vanilla, if using. Leave to stand for 1–2 hours.

In a large mixing bowl, whisk egg yolks and sugar until pale and thick. Scald cream mixture and pour gradually onto yolks and sugar, whisking all the time. Pour this new custard mixture into the saucepan and cook gently, stirring continuously, until the custard thickens. It will not thicken much because there are not a lot of yolks, so take care not to boil and curdle it. When lots of tiny bubbles appear on the surface and it swells a little, it is time to stop cooking. Pour through a sieve to remove vanilla beans, and set aside to cool before processing in an icecream maker.

Poached peaches

6 medium-sized peaches
water to cover
8 oz/220 g sugar

Place peaches in a saucepan and cover with water. Add sugar, bring to a boil, and simmer gently until peaches are tender enough for the point of a sharp knife to pierce easily through to the pit (stone). When done, hold under cold water then peel skins off. Place in a serving bowl with some of the cooking syrup and chill.

Jenny's puff pastry

This is best made when you have a few hours' spare. Store it in the freezer and use as required.

2 8-oz/250-g blocks salted butter
1 lb/500 g plain (all-purpose) flour
about 12 fl oz/375 ml iced water
pinch salt

Let butter soften to room temperature—it should be neither hard nor too soft.

Sift flour into a bowl and add water, little by little, until it makes a pliable dough. Rest in refrigerator for 20 minutes before continuing.

Roll dough out into a rectangle about 24 x 8 in (60 x 20 cm). Slice blocks of butter in half lengthwise. Place the four sticks of butter, long edge to long edge, in the lower half of the dough rectangle, leaving an edge of dough all the way around. Fold the top half of the dough over, and press the edges firmly together all the way around to enclose the butter in a parcel. Hit the parcel with the rolling pin to start flattening it, then roll out away from you, flattening the butter inside as you do. You may need to flour the board and pin, so that the pastry doesn't stick—brush off any excess flour with a brush. Be careful not to let the butter break through the parcel at any stage, but if it does, patch the hole, and brush with a little flour.

Turn the pastry package 90° anti-clockwise, so that the pressed edge is at your right, and the folded edge at your left, as though you were about to open a book.

Roll out to full size again, and fold as before, turn, press the edges together, roll out, fold, press edges, and turn. Wrap in foil, and rest in the refrigerator for 20 minutes before continuing (if the weather is very hot, the dough will need to rest longer).

Repeat this folding procedure four more times. (At this stage you can wrap the pastry in plastic and store in the freezer for later use).

Fresh (unfrozen) pastry should rest for 20 minutes before using.

A romantic dinner for two

A romantic dinner for two

Ornamental Frosted Fruits

~

Apple and Parsnip Soup

~

Hearts of Salmon

~

Champagne Sorbet

~

Herb-Crusted Lamb Roast with Vegetables

~

Figs Stuffed with Ricotta and Pistachio Nuts

~

Coffee and Chocolates

*r*omance can be dangerous. So too, it seems, can knowledge. When Adam and Eve tasted the forbidden fruit in the Garden of Eden, they were cast out of Paradise. Rudely awoken from their innocence, they became aware of their differences and stitched together fig leaves to hide their nakedness. So began the long dance.

Just what that fruit was is not revealed. Traditionally, it has been thought to be an apple, although there is no evidence for that and apples, as we know them, probably didn't grow in ancient Palestine. Perhaps it was a "divine" fruit, unique to the Garden of Eden? For me, figs are a divine fruit. Soft, sweet, pink-bellied, and ambrosial, they have long been surrounded by an aura of sexuality. Along with grapes, they were one of the few plants to survive the last Ice Age. And where would we be without the grape? No wine. No champagne. No tear-shaped black and green beauties waiting to be popped in the mouth or peeled by an obliging lover. Peeling grapes, by the way, is fine but never peel a fig—eat it with the fingers, skin and all.

Seductive food

At this romantic dinner for two, we have worked around the Adam and Eve myth (for who can resist what is specifically forbidden). A number of the fruits thought to have been grown in the Garden are the focal piece of the table and are also included in the recipes: apple in the apple and parsnip soup, grapes in the champagne, wines, and sorbet, and figs for the dessert. This is a little more subtle than relying on the usual aphrodisiacs such as caviar, oysters, truffles, and chocolate.

The search for the ultimate aphrodisiac is indeed as old as history—perhaps that's why Eve was tempted to sample the forbidden fruit. The tastes, textures and physical characteristics of some foods hint of sexual pleasure. Their very appearance may be highly stimulating. Think of asparagus, mussels, ripe figs, eggs, and the sensual opportunities they offer both in the presentation and in the eating. And there are others, like parsley, young parsnips, and carrot tops, that have a more subtle pheromonal effect.

Falling in love is delicious and frightening—this dinner should be the former and definitely not the latter. There is to be no gnawing on bones, no slurping or dripping of juices, no wind-producing beans, no savaging of ripe fruits.

Consider not only the type of food and its presentation with the occasional dash of sexual allusion here and there, but the lightness of each dish. No heavy sauces, no foods that are difficult to digest or weigh down the stomach.

Preparing ahead

Essential to the evening's success is the planning and organization of the meal. Your goal should be the minimum of cooking at the last minute, and if you follow

also set the table the day (or night) before. Choose an elegant cloth with matching napkins, your best cutlery, glasses, plates, and candle holders. Have an ice bucket ready for the champagne and check that you have sufficient ice in the freezer. Chill the champagne and white wine in the refrigerator, and have the red wine ready to be opened. Pop a couple of glasses into the freezer, ready to fill with the sorbet. Check your salt and pepper shakers. Are your candles in good condition? Make sure they will last through the night. And music? I'd suggest Ella Fitzgerald singing Jerome Kern or Joao Gilberto and Antonio Carlos Jobim playing their beautiful Brazilian pieces. Whatever you choose, make sure everything (including yourself) is ready as soon as there's a knock on the door, or a key in the lock.

this menu, you should be able to prepare just about everything ahead. The lamb is the only item requiring last-minute cooking but is a well-tempered dish and requires little concern or attention. The soup and vegetables will need warming. The soup, mousse, and sorbet can be prepared the day before; the vegetables, sugared fruits, dressing for the salmon, lamb, and figs can be done on the day. Coffee takes little preparation—serve it with heart-shaped chocolates and silver almonds to finish the dinner. Read through this menu and each recipe carefully beforehand; the food should appear effortlessly and with little fuss.

If your partner for this dinner is not around, you can

Wine suggestions

~ As an aperitif, perhaps with the frosted fruits: kir made with créme de cassis and a light, simple sparkling wine such as Crémant de Loire.

~ With the soup: a delicate, dry riesling, such as a German trocken style, a New Zealand or Alsatian riesling.

~ With the lamb roast: a fruity young cabernet-based red of a lighter style, such as Bourgueil or Chinon, a lighter Bordeaux or cool-grown New World cabernet.

~ With coffee and chocolates: Cognac, of at least VSOP grade but preferably an XO or deluxe blend.

"The greatest love is the love of food."

George Bernard Shaw

Frosted fruits

These are used as an edible table decoration.

clusters of green and black grapes
perfect green apples
perfect green figs
fig leaves
grape leaves
2 egg whites
caster (superfine) sugar

Wash fruit and leaves and dry well. Whisk egg whites until frothy, not stiff. Pour sugar onto a plate. Dip fruit first into egg white, making sure it is well but lightly coated, then sprinkle liberally with sugar. Let dry on trays covered with waxed (greaseproof) paper. The leaves can also be dipped, following the same procedure. Assemble fruits on a beautiful glass stand, with leaves interspersed.

Apple and parsnip soup

Prepare this ahead, and gently warm it before serving. You can swirl in a little cream, if you like.

1 large green apple, about 6 oz/180 g, peeled and cored
1 creamy parsnip, about 8 oz/250 g, peeled and chopped
1/8 teaspoon curry powder
20 fl oz/600 ml chicken stock
salt and white pepper
slivered peel from 1/2 green apple for garnish

Place apple and parsnip in a saucepan, add curry powder, and cover with stock. Bring to a boil and simmer gently until tender. Blend in a food processor or blender until smooth, and season to taste. Can be prepared ahead up to this point.

Return to heat and simmer gently until hot. Just before serving, garnish with the slivered peel from the green apple.

apple and parsnip soup

Hearts of salmon

Remove the sorbet from the refrigerator as you serve the salmon—this will give it time to soften.

For the molds
2 coeur à la crème molds
vegetable oil or non-stick spray
4 slices smoked salmon, about 3½ oz/100 g

For the mousse
½ sachet (⅙ oz/5 g) gelatin
2 tablespoons cold water
4 oz/125 g good-quality canned salmon, drained and boned
dash brandy
salt and white pepper
1 teaspoon chopped fresh dill
¼ cup (2 fl oz/60 ml) thickened cream, lightly whipped
1 egg white, stiffly beaten

For the dressing
juice of 2 limes
1 tablespoon light olive oil
pinch sea salt
freshly ground black pepper
1 teaspoon finely chopped chives

*L*ightly brush insides of molds with vegetable oil. Press plastic wrap into molds so that it sits evenly. Drape 2 slices of salmon over each mold, pressing into the sides to give a good shape. Refrigerate until mousse is ready.

In a small bowl, dissolve gelatin in water and whisk until dissolved (if you set this over a bowl of hot water, it helps the gelatin to dissolve more quickly). Place dissolved gelatin and salmon in a food processor, and process until smooth. Spoon into a mixing bowl. Add brandy, salt, pepper, and dill, and stir well to combine. Fold through cream and then egg white.

Spoon into the prepared molds and fold the smoked salmon pieces over to form a neat package. Cover each with plastic wrap and refrigerate for a couple of hours. Any additional mousse can be stored for use another time. The hearts can be prepared ahead up to this point.

Before serving, combine all dressing ingredients in a bowl and whisk well to combine. Turn each heart out carefully onto a small plate. Spoon dressing over.

Champagne sorbet

Although this sorbet is at its best eaten on the day it is made, you can make it the day before and it will still be good.

8 oz/250 g sugar
8 fl oz/250 ml water
8 fl oz/250 ml champagne
juice of ½ lemon
3½ fl oz/100 ml mineral water

*B*ring sugar and water to boil in a saucepan, stirring to dissolve sugar, and then simmer for 5 minutes. Remove and cool. Mix this sugar syrup with champagne, lemon juice, and mineral water. Chill in the refrigerator.

Churn in an icecream machine, following manufacturer's instructions for best results. (Or freeze, then beat, re-freeze and re-beat 3 times at 20 minute intervals.) Store in freezer in covered container. Remove from refrigerator 15 minutes before serving to allow to soften a little. Spoon into glasses which have been chilled in the freezer.

champagne sorbet

herb-crusted lamb roast

Herb-crusted lamb roast

1 lamb topside roast, about 12 oz/375 g (trim lamb preferred)
1 small clove garlic, slivered
salt and freshly ground pepper
1 tablespoon olive oil

For the herb crust
1 tablespoon Dijon mustard
1 tablespoon light soy sauce
1 oz/30 g chopped fresh mixed herbs (parsley, rosemary, sage, basil)

Wipe meat dry with paper towels, insert slivers of garlic at various points with a small sharp knife. Season with salt and pepper. Heat oil in a pan and sear the meat on all sides. Remove and cool.

Process mustard, soy sauce, and herbs in a food processor until herbs are finely chopped. Transfer to a bowl. Dip the top and sides of the roast in the herb mixture. Can be pre-prepared up to this stage.

Cook in oven preheated to 400°F (200°C/Gas 6) for 18–20 minutes. Remove and cover with foil. Let rest 10 minutes before carving. Serve with natural juices from the lamb or deglaze the pan with a little red wine.

Vegetables

4 baby carrots, peeled, with a little of the green top left intact
4 small spring onions, peeled with a little of the green top
    left intact
4 baby squash, washed
4 fat asparagus spears, sliced diagonally in 4-in (10-cm)
    lengths
1 oz/30 g butter, melted

Steam the vegetables until al dente, putting carrots and onions in first and cooking for 3–4 minutes, then adding squash and asparagus and cooking a further 2–3 minutes. The vegetables can be prepared ahead up to this point and kept covered in the refrigerator or at room temperature for a few hours.

Just before serving, warm and glaze them by tossing in melted butter in a frying pan.

Figs stuffed with ricotta and pistachio nuts

Never peel figs! Eat them skins and all. As the perfect and intimate climax to this meal, you could try feeding them to each other with your hands. You will probably only want to eat one between you, but make two just in case.

2 perfect fresh black figs, gently washed and dried
10 fresh pistachio nuts, shelled and slivered

For the stuffing
4 oz/125 g ricotta
1 tablespoon creme de cassis (blackcurrant liqueur)
1 tablespoon caster (superfine) sugar
2 tablespoons thickened or whipping cream

For the syrup
4 oz/110 g caster (superfine) sugar
2 fl oz/60 ml water
1 tablespoon creme de cassis

Slice figs in half just through to the stem, being careful not to cut all the way through, then slice again into quarters. Open them out to form four petals.

Put ricotta into a small bowl and mash with a fork. Add cassis and sugar and combine well, then stir in cream and beat until well combined. Fill each fig with ricotta mixture, then gently push the petals back up to form a flower. You can prepare the figs ahead to this point.

Bring sugar and water to a boil in a small saucepan, stirring to dissolve the sugar. Add cassis and simmer until the syrup reduces and forms a fairly sticky consistency. Leave to cool slightly.

Just before serving, drizzle warm syrup over figs and scatter pistachio nuts on top.

figs stuffed with ricotta and pistachio nuts

A midsummer night's theme

A midsummer night's theme

Serves 8-10

B'Stilla

~

Baked Whole Fish in Chermoula

Couscous

Salads
*Chilled Carrot Salad ~ Hot and Spicy Carrot Salad
~ Beet Salad ~ Radish Salad ~ Eggplant Petal Salad*

~

Chilled Orange Slices
Moroccan Date and Fig Slice

*C*an one dinner affect your life? Can it so haunt you that for years the very scent of a spice or flower reminds you of it? Maybe. Especially if it's on a midsummer's night, a time of year that ushers in its own kind of magic. I remember one such dinner many years ago. It was held outdoors on a terrace under a pergola of cool green leaves. The terrace itself overlooked the ocean and as evening fell, a full orange moon rose from under the sea and up into the slowly darkening sky. As it climbed higher, it lost its orange hue and gradually turned silver.

The beauty of the evening and the display of the moon were, of course, completely out of our hands. But we did have control over a few of the elements, namely the setting, the theme, and the food.

The setting
A round table covered with a tablecloth and strewn with rose petals; on the table a brass tray filled with exotic fruits such as pomegranates, figs, and fresh dates, and surrounding this, small votive candles; in the trees, garlands of fairy lights; and in the background, the faint sound of a fountain. The theme, Moroccan.

Occasionally, when entertaining, it is a good idea to choose a theme around which to build your party. You don't have to inform guests of your intentions unless you would like them to dress in keeping with the theme, and send out invitations that encourage them to do so. Providing a different sort of experience for your guests, something to inspire the imagination, can add to the enjoyment of the evening. The entire affair can be original, sophisticated, and stylish without stooping to gimmickry or ostentation.

When well stage-managed, such a dinner can unfold in a series of delights and surprises. Try not to be too rigid about it though—people become intimidated if everything is so perfectly planned and plotted that there is no room for spontaneity.

Lighting is important. Use it carefully and creatively to cast intricate patterns and shadows on your table and transform your garden into a magical place. A very good effect can be created by fairy lights in the trees (keep them all the same) and by candles on the table, either the squat, votive kind or candelabras—they cast a flattering light onto food, china, glass, and people's faces. Candles placed inside waxed paper bags and positioned along a pathway or in a courtyard have a similarly mellowing effect. The bags can be partly filled with sand to steady the candle and hold the bag in place. Add citronella to burning candles (or use citronella candles) to add a lovely fresh scent and to keep insects at bay; mosquito coils are also effective repellents.

Fragrance is also important. Aromas from plants like gardenias, tuber roses, freesias, and jasmine wafting gently on the night breeze can seduce and enchant. If you don't have them growing in your garden, fill jars with cuttings or float flowers in bowls of water.

Keep the number of guests small —eight is ideal. That way everyone has a chance to speak to each other. If you can, seat them at a round table so that all the guests can see and hear each other. You'll probably find the atmosphere more convivial and the conversation thoughtful and informed. A good host will endeavour to bring together a variety of wit and talent. Dinner parties profit from a little controversy and unpredictability, so invite people from different walks of life.

Food with mood

When choosing the menu, surprise your guests. Be adventurous but realistic. Like your surroundings, the meal itself should carry the theme. Moroccan food offers a wonderful opportunity to introduce sweet and savory tastes and to present something a little unusual—such as the B'stilla in our menu. If you start with that dish, move on to the fish and salads, and then to the fruit desserts, you are offering a range of taste, texture, and appearance that will appeal to both eye and palate. In her classic book on Moroccan cooking, Paula Wolfert says that B'stilla "is so intricate, so lavish and so rich, that its extravagance always reminds me of The Arabian Nights." It's fun to add something new to your repertoire, and this Moroccan delight is not to be found in any other country.

If you are attempting a completely new dish you might like to try it out first on your family or close friends. It's a good idea to check the ingredients and cooking time and become familiar with them. You can then add your own personal touch and variations to the recipe.

The B'stilla can be prepared well ahead and frozen. You only need to take it out on the morning of the dinner to defrost and reheat before serving. Give it another dusting of icing sugar and cinnamon before doing so. Even the couscous can be prepared ahead and frozen. The salad vegetables can be prepared in the morning and stored in separate containers, covered tightly, in the refrigerator. Keep the sliced radishes in a bowl of water, and drain and dress them later in the day. The cooked carrots too need dressing with oil only at the last moment or they will become slimy. The chermoula—a spicy Moroccon marinade used here with baked fish—can be prepared the day before, so that only the fish itself will need cooking; watch it carefully so that it does not overcook. Prepare the sliced oranges on the day. The fruit slice keeps for weeks. You will notice orange blossom water is used in many of these recipes; it is a central ingredient in Arabic cooking and can be purchased from specialist food stores.

This menu also makes the shift from kitchen to an outdoor setting easy. The B'stilla and couscous are served warm, the salads are cold. The only hot dish is the fish, which can be covered with foil for its journey to the table. If it is a long journey, think about setting up a side table to use for both serving and clearing, and a container with ice to keep wine chilled.

If you are well organized in this way, you can enjoy your own party.

b'stilla

"Here let us feast, and to the feast be join'd discourse,
the sweeter banquet of the mind."

- Pope, *Homer*

Wine suggestions

~*With the B'stilla:* a rich chardonnay, such as a white Burgundy from Meursault or Californian from the Napa Valley.

~*With the fish:* a soft but dry rosé, preferably from Bandol or Provence.

B'stilla

For the chicken

4lb/2 kg chicken thighs and legs
6 stalks fresh coriander (cilantro)
2 large onions, grated or finely chopped in food processor
2 bay leaves
1 tablespoon freshly grated ginger
1 teaspoon freshly ground black pepper
1/4 teaspoon saffron threads
1/4 teaspoon turmeric
3 cinnamon sticks
1 teaspoon salt
24 fl oz/750 ml water
4 oz/125 g butter
pinch ground ginger, optional

For the almonds

2 tablespoons peanut oil
1 lb/500 g whole blanched almonds
2 teaspoons cinnamon
3 tablespoons icing (powdered) sugar
1 tablespoon orange blossom water
2 tablespoons rosewater
2 oz/60 g softened butter, cut into pieces

For the egg mixture

4 fl oz/125 ml lemon juice
10 eggs, well beaten
1/2 bunch flat-leaf (Italian/continental) parsley, chopped
1/2 teaspoon salt

For the pie crust

5 oz/150 g clarified butter, melted
2 tablespoons orange blossom water
8 oz/250 g filo pastry

icing (powdered) sugar
cinnamon

Combine all ingredients for the chicken, except the ground ginger, in a large pan, cover, and bring to a boil. Lower the heat and simmer for 1 hour, stirring occasionally.

While chicken cooks, prepare the almond layer. Heat oil in a large frying pan, and brown almonds lightly in two batches. Drain well on paper towels. When cool, chop roughly. You can do this in the food processor but be careful not to overprocess. Quickly blend in cinnamon, icing sugar, orange blossom water, rosewater, and butter, and set aside.

Remove chicken pieces from pan, put into a bowl, and set aside to cool. Discard cinnamon sticks and any loose bones from the remaining liquid, and bring this to a boil, reducing to 1 1/2 cups (12 fl oz/375 ml). Lower heat until simmering and add lemon juice. Pour in eggs, add parsley, and stir constantly over medium heat until eggs are cooked—they should be curdy, but not dry. Add salt to taste. Spread on a baking sheet to cool.

Shred chicken, removing skin, bones, and gristle. Adjust seasoning, and add ground ginger, if desired. Set aside.

Preheat oven to 425°F (220°C/Gas 7). Prepare the pie crust by mixing together butter and orange blossom water. Brush a little of the butter over the base of an 11–12 in (27.5–30 cm) cake pan, pizza pan, or paella dish. Cover with a sheet of pastry. Lightly brush with the butter–orange blossom mixture. Drape another 5–6 sheets over the pan, overlapping them so they cover the base completely, and brushing each one with the butter–orange blossom mixture. The pastry leaves should extend beyond the sides of the pan so they can be folded up and in later.

Strew almond mixture over entire base of pastry-lined pan, then lay 3 sheets pastry, each sheet brushed with butter, over the top. Strew chicken over this layer, then lay another 3 layers of pastry over the top. If you fold each sheet of pastry in half, brushing with butter as you go, it gives a firmer layer. Spoon egg mixture over.

Cover with 2 pastry leaves, folded in half and buttered, to make a firm top. Fold the extended pastry leaves over the top of the pie to cover and enclose. Place another 4–5 buttered leaves on top, tucking them in around the edges to make a neat package. Brush with more butter, drizzling some down the sides of the pan.

Bake 15 minutes in the middle of the pre-heated oven. Remove from oven and use a spatula to loosen pie around the edges. Invert onto a large lightly greased baking sheet, and return to oven for a further 20 minutes until golden brown all over.

Remove from oven and dust with icing sugar and cinnamon. To make a decorative pattern on top, first dust with icing sugar. Cut out strips of waxed (greaseproof) paper and lay in a criss-cross pattern over the top. Sprinkle over the cinnamon to give a striped effect.

baked whole fish in chermoula

Baked whole fish in chermoula

1 whole snapper, about 4 lb/2 kg, cleaned, scaled, washed, and dried

For the chermoula
2 bunches fresh coriander (cilantro)
1 bunch flat-leaf (Italian/continental) parsley
6 cloves garlic, peeled and crushed
salt to taste
2 tablespoons cumin
2 tablespoons paprika
1/2 teaspoon cayenne pepper
3 1/2 oz/100 ml lemon juice
8 fl oz/250 ml olive oil

To cook
2 long stalks celery, sliced
8 fl oz/250 ml dry white wine, or water
1 large red onion, sliced into rings
1 green capsicum (bell pepper), seeded and sliced into rings
2 ripe tomatoes, sliced
2 preserved lemons, cut in quarters and flesh removed
18 large green or violet olives

Slash the fish diagonally in 2 or 3 places on both sides. Make the chermoula: chop herbs together until fine, add garlic and salt; stir through the remaining chermoula ingredients, mixing well to combine.

Put half the chermoula inside the cavity of the fish, and rub the remaining half into the skin and slits of the fish. Leave to marinate for 2 hours.

Preheat oven to 400°F (200°C/Gas 6).

Scatter the celery over the bottom of a baking dish large enough to fit the whole fish. Pour in wine and lay the fish in the dish. Strew onion, capsicum, and tomatoes over the top. Cover tightly with foil and bake 30–35 minutes. Reduce oven to 350°F (180°C/Gas 4), remove foil, and bake a further 10–15 minutes or until fish is cooked and tomatoes have dried out a little. To test if fish is cooked, insert a sharp knife into the thickest part of the flesh around the head—the flesh should be white and flaky. Garnish fish with preserved lemon skins and olives.

Couscous

Use pre-soaked couscous for ease of preparation. Serve it piled up in a Moroccan tagine if you have access to one.

24 fl oz/750 ml boiling water
1½ lb/750 g couscous
1 14-oz (440-g) can chickpeas, drained
6 oz/185 g seedless raisins or sultanas (golden raisins)
3½ oz/100 g slivered almonds, toasted
4 oz/125 g butter
2 teaspoons cumin
1 teaspoon ground coriander
1 teaspoon salt

Pour boiling water over couscous in a large bowl. Leave to soak for 10 minutes. Add chick peas, dried fruit, and almonds, and stir to combine. Melt butter in a large frying pan. Add couscous and stir in spices and salt. Keep stirring until butter is evenly dispersed through couscous and grains are separated.

Hot and spicy carrot salad

Harissa is a hot Moroccan red pepper sauce. If unavailable, substitute with sambal oelek or cayenne.

2 lb/1 kg medium carrots, peeled
1 clove garlic, peeled and halved
2 fl oz/60 ml lemon juice
1 teaspoon cumin
1 teaspoon paprika
½ teaspoon harissa
½ teaspoon cayenne pepper
½ teaspoon cinnamon
½ teaspoon sugar
salt
olive oil
freshly chopped flat-leaf (Italian/continental) parsley,
  for garnish

Cook carrots with garlic in a large pan of boiling water until carrots are just tender. Drain, and cut them into halves lengthwise.

Mix together lemon juice and spices, seasoning with salt. Combine well and pour over carrots, tossing them in the mixture until well coated. Cool to room temperature, cover, and refrigerate.

Just before serving, sprinkle salad with olive oil and toss well. Garnish with parsley.

Chilled carrot salad

This is excellent for cleansing the palate after the B'stilla and fish.

juice of 4–6 oranges
4 large carrots, peeled and coarsely grated
caster (superfine) sugar, if needed
about ¼ teaspoon cinnamon or to taste

In a salad bowl, pour orange juice over the carrots. Add a little sugar if the oranges aren't sweet. Sprinkle with cinnamon. Cover with plastic wrap, and chill well before serving.

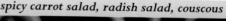

spicy carrot salad, radish salad, couscous

Beet salad

When trimming the beets, don't cut the skin, otherwise the juices will "bleed" during cooking.

2 lb/1 kg fresh beets (beetroot), leaves trimmed off
1 medium red onion, cut in large cubes
juice of 1 lemon
4 fl oz/125 ml olive oil
salt
zest of 1 orange, finely grated
1 tablespoon orange blossom water
2 tablespoons chopped fresh parsley
2 tablespoons chopped fresh coriander (cilantro)

Cook beets in boiling salted water until tender; a knife or skewer should pierce them easily. Drain. Slip off skins while still warm—this is best done under cold running water. Cut into cubes and put into a salad bowl.

Mix together remaining ingredients. Toss well with beets and adjust seasoning.

Radish salad

2 bunches radishes, trimmed and thinly sliced
juice of 1/2 lemon
juice of 1/2 orange
1 tablespoon orange blossom water
pinch sugar
pinch salt
olive oil

In a salad bowl combine radishes with citrus juices and orange blossom water, and mix through sugar and salt. Just before serving, drizzle with olive oil.

Eggplant petal salad

Buy finger-length baby black eggplants (aubergine) for this salad.

1 1/2 lb/750 g baby eggplants (aubergine)
salt
2 fl oz/60 ml olive oil
juice of 1/2 lemon
good pinch cayenne pepper
1 teaspoon cumin

Cut each eggplant in half lengthwise to stem end, then cut each half lengthwise again into quarters, leaving the stem end uncut and the eggplant looking like a four-petalled flower. Sprinkle eggplants with salt and leave in a colander to drain juices for 1–2 hours. Rinse well.

Bring a large pan of water to a boil and cook eggplants in gently simmering water for 10–15 minutes or until soft but not mushy. Drain and squeeze out any excess moisture.

In a small bowl, mix together oil, lemon juice, cayenne pepper, and cumin. Brush each "petal" with this mixture. Arrange in decorative fashion on a platter and serve with the fish.

Moroccan date and fig slice

This can be made well ahead as it keeps well. In the heat of summer it is best to keep it refrigerated.

1 lb/500 g dried Smyrna figs
1 lb/500 g pitted (stoned) dates, diced
8 oz/250 g pecans, coarsely chopped
3 fl oz/80 ml Grand Marnier or other orange liqueur
zest of 1 orange, finely grated
3–4 tablespoons honey

Process figs in a food processor until fairly small but not mushy; alternatively, use a knife and cut into small dice. Mix figs in a bowl with remaining ingredients. Line a loaf pan with plastic wrap and fill with the mixture. Press down very firmly until compacted. Cover, and chill in refrigerator for a couple of hours. Turn out onto a serving plate and remove plastic wrap. Use a sharp knife to slice as needed.

Chilled orange slices

10–12 large best-quality oranges, peeled, pith and membrane removed, sliced into circles
6–8 fresh dates, halved, pitted (stoned), and slivered
rosewater
cinnamon
icing (powdered) sugar

Arrange orange circles in a salad bowl in overlapping circles. Strew dates over oranges. Sprinkle with rosewater, cover with plastic wrap, and chill. Just before serving, dust lightly with cinnamon and sugar.

Moroccan date and fig slice

chilled orange slices

"*A yellow-coated pomegranate, figs like lizard's necks,*
a handful of half-rosy part-ripe grapes,
a quince all delicate-downed and fragrant fleeced,
a walnut winking out from its green shell,
a cucumber with the bloom on it pouting from its leaf-bed,
and a ripe gold-coated olive"

Philip of Thessalonika c. AD40

133

A child's party

A child's party

Serves 12

Choice of

Mini Pizza Faces

Mini Carrot and Currant Muffins

~

Egg Toadstools

Mini Vegetables

~

Choice of

Meringue Icecream Cones

Mushroom Meringues

Fairy Bread

Enchanted Mushrooms

Face Cookies

Sultana Loaf

~

Choice of

Jigsaw Puzzle

Toffee Apples

Fruit Salad Ices

~

Basket of Strawberries Birthday Cake

*i*t's that time of year again. Comes around so quickly that sometimes it can feel as though you've only just recovered from one birthday to face another, especially if you have more than one child.

If that's the case, you could try alternating so that a child has a party every second year: my son is given a party one year, my daughter has hers the following year. Be careful to keep a record—crafty children may swear they didn't have a party the year before, and try to coax and sway you. Limiting the number of celebrations in this way makes them manageable and makes sense for busy parents. You can then put your best effort into the party and not end up feeling too dazed and frazzled.

Children usually want to invite all their friends. Only you will know how many you can cope with, but if you keep the numbers small (twelve would be the maximum), limit the hours, and plan some fun games, you may even be able to enjoy yourself as well.

Planning the party

At our house, the anticipation begins to build a few weeks prior with the issuing of invitations. Over the years, I have tried to encourage the children to design their own, rather than buy ready-made ones. The more personal the invitations are, the better. As well, it gives the children a sense of really contributing to their birthday and sparks off their enthusiasm. Make sure all the details are included—starting and finishing times, address, date, and if it's fancy dress.

Children love to dress up and a fancy dress or costume party inspires their imaginations, so why not plan your party around a theme? This party with Peter Rabbit has been designed for four to seven year olds and is based on ones I have given at different times for both my son and daughter. The children are asked to come dressed as rabbits and foxes. But no prizes for best-dressed—it causes too much anguish, and children could end up in tears if they don't win.

The best parties for this age group are short—about two hours is ideal. The earlier in the day the party is held, the more likely it is to be successful as the children will be livelier. Around noon is a good time to start, although some prefer to start as late as 3.30 pm. Warn the people next door and put pets away. Store valuables where they cannot be harmed. On the day, hang a few balloons on your front door or gate to mark it for those guests who haven't been to your home before. They also lend a festive air to the celebrations.

Decorate the table or tables as prettily as you can and keep them a secret—if you can—until unveiled. If you are holding the party indoors and have a room you can darken, pull the curtains, light the candles and then call the children.

Fun food

Prepare as much as you can in advance and avoid things that require last minute work. Choose food that looks interesting and novel and that is easy to eat and serve. Try using mini-vegetables as holders for place cards on the table. Balance the treats with healthy food, and try to find out if any of the children are on special diets. At this age, they love food they can pick up in their fingers, so keep everything small—mini muffins, mini pizzas, mini vegetables. If you run out of ideas for food, mini pies and burgers, and cocktail frankfurters are always popular. Even if they are well past toddler stage, the feel and texture of food is still very appealing. Set aside a platter of sandwiches or antipasto for other parents to nibble on when they come to pick up their children. A couple of extra adults on hand won't go astray, and they might just help you with some of the games or winding-up activities.

If you're holding the party inside, consider setting it up in the kitchen if there is enough room. It is easier to remove food and stains from a hard surface than from a carpeted one. If you have to risk your carpet, cover it with paper or plastic to minimize any damage and make cleaning easier.

Fun and games

Work out a time schedule for events beforehand. Start with a few games and offer the children mini pizza faces and mini muffins. Make sure the children know where the bathroom is. If you have an outdoor area, have the children play outdoor games for a while, letting them run around and be silly before they sit down to eat properly—this will rouse their appetites and

dissipate some of the initial excitement. Once seated, offer them egg toadstools and mini vegetables, then the rest of the treats, leaving the jigsaw puzzle and toffee apples until the end of the party. If they aren't eaten, they can be wrapped up along with a piece of birthday cake for the children to take home (wrap the toffee apples in foil).

Later, get them to play some quieter games, such as "pass the parcel" or "Beatrix Potter quiz" (see our suggestion box), which will help settle them into a reasonably calm state before their parents arrive. Keep competitive games to a minimum as they only cause pouting and tears, and try to ensure that every child goes home with a small gift.

Set aside some time for your child to open presents, and make sure the child thanks friends for their gifts, either at the time or later by way of a note or telephone call. Birthday parties are an important way of learning social graces and instilling etiquette, even if it seems hard to believe in the midst of the hullabaloo.

mini pizza faces

Mini pizza faces

16 slices brown or wholewheat (wholemeal) bread
olive oil
tomato paste (purée)
pimento-stuffed olives, sliced thinly
button mushrooms (champignons), sliced thinly
3–4 small ripe tomatoes
grated cheddar cheese
alfalfa sprouts

Stamp out rounds of bread with a cutter, 3-in (7.5-cm) across, and toast lightly. Brush slices with a little olive oil and then spread with tomato paste. Make faces, using olives for eyes and mushrooms for ears. For mouths, slice tomatoes and cut slices into halves. Sprinkle with grated cheese. Heat under hot grill (broiler) to melt the cheese if desired. Serve pizza faces on alfalfa sprouts on a tray or in a basket.

Mini carrot and currant muffins

Makes 36 bite-size muffins

Bake a dried bean in one of the muffins, and whoever finds it, gets a prize—but make sure you first tell the children not to eat it. Use mini muffin pans so that the muffins are small enough for the children to eat them in one or two bites.

4 oz/125 g plain (all-purpose) flour
2 oz/60 g oat bran
1 teaspoon bicarbonate of soda (baking soda)
1 teaspoon cinnamon
1/4 teaspoon salt
2 eggs
4 oz/125 g brown sugar
2 tablespoons vegetable oil
1 teaspoon vanilla essence/extract
2 1/2 oz/75 g carrot, grated
2 oz/60 g currants
icing (powdered) sugar

*P*reheat oven to 350°F (180°C/Gas 4). Lightly grease the muffin pans.

Sift flour and mix with other dry ingredients in a large mixing bowl.

In another bowl, beat eggs and sugar. When light and fluffy, whisk in oil and vanilla. Stir in carrots and currants, and pour this mixture over dry ingredients. Fold lightly until dry ingredients are just moist. Spoon batter into muffin pans and bake for 15 minutes or until golden and firm to the touch. Turn out onto a cake rack to cool. Dust lightly with icing sugar.

Egg toadstools

The eggs can be cooked a day ahead, then finished off as toadstools on the morning of the party, but keep them refrigerated. You can make a paper piping bag to pipe the mayonnaise (see glossary). If the children don't like salami, you can substitute tomato: choose two large ripe tomatoes and slice them down their sides to give four "lids" from each tomato, and top the eggs with these.

8 hard-boiled eggs
24 small slices salami
2–3 tablespoons mayonnaise
parsley sprigs

*S*lice bottoms off eggs so they sit straight, then slice off tops. Place three salami slices in overlapping circles on top. Using the paper piping bag, pipe small dots of mayonnaise on the top of salami. Stand the eggs on a plate surrounded with fresh parsley.

Mini vegetables

Prepare these on the morning of the party and store in an airtight container until ready to use. Keep refrigerated.

2–3 large carrots, peeled
1 cucumber, sliced
8 tear-drop tomatoes
8 cherry tomatoes

*U*sing aspic- or mini-cutters, cut carrots into pretty shapes. Cut cucumber slices into halves. Halve tomatoes. Combine vegetable shapes and place in small bowls along with egg toadstools.

egg toadstools

meringue icecream cones

rosettes in the shape of an icecream. Sprinkle with chocolate sprinkles or hundreds and thousands, and bake for 1 hour. Turn off oven, and leave meringues inside to cool slightly. Remove from paper and finish cooling on a rack.

Melt chocolate in a bowl over hot water. Dip edges of cones in chocolate, place a meringue rosette on top of each cone. Stand the cones upright—in a holder or in cups—and leave to set.

Mushroom meringues

*T*o make "mushroom meringues", line a baking sheet with non-stick baking paper (parchment). Using an icing bag fitted with a ¹/₂-in (1-cm) plain icing tube, pipe small meringue mounds of various sizes for the mushroom caps, and an equal number of small cone-shaped mounds for the stems. Flatten any sharp points on caps with a finger dipped in water. Dust some of the caps with cocoa powder. Bake in oven preheated to 250°F (120°C/Gas 1/2) for 30 minutes. Cool on racks. With the tip of a sharp knife,

Meringues

This recipe makes enough meringue for 12 "icecream cones" and lots of "mushroom meringues".

5 oz/150 g egg whites
10 oz/300 g caster (superfine) sugar
chocolate sprinkles or hundreds and thousands
3¹/₂ oz/100 g unsweetened cooking chocolate
12 packaged icecream cones
cocoa powder

*P*reheat oven to 250°F (120 °C/Gas 1/2). Whip egg whites until foamy, then gradually add 7 oz/200 g of the sugar. Continue whipping until very firm and shiny. Sift remaining sugar over mixture, carefully folding into the whites with a rubber spatula.

Icecream cones

*L*ine a baking sheet with non-stick parchment (baking paper). Using a small cutter or circular object, mark 12 circles in pencil as close to the size of the diameter of the top of the icecream cones as possible. Using an icing bag fitted with a small fluted icing tube, pipe meringue in large

scrape out meringue on the underside of the caps to make small holes. Dip tips of mushroom stems into melted chocolate and press stems into holes of caps. Leave to set.

Face cookies

Use the icing left over from the jigsaw puzzle cake for making these cute faces.

royal icing (see recipe on page 142)
blue and red food dyes
16 oval sweet biscuits (e.g. Arrowroot)
candy such as M & Ms, Smarties
shredded coconut
cachous

D ivide icing in two and place in separate bowls. Add a few drops of different food dye to each bowl and stir well to combine. Spread icing evenly over the biscuit tops using a small spatula. Decorate with candy, shredded coconut, and cachous to make pretty faces.

mushroom meringues

face cookies

Fairy bread

This needs to be made on the day as it will dry out if made any earlier. Store in an airtight container until just before serving.

softened butter
8 slices white bread
hundreds and thousands

S pread butter lightly on bread and sprinkle evenly all over with hundreds and thousands. Use cookie cutters to stamp out different shapes (butterflies, angels, moons, and stars).

Enchanted mushrooms

softened butter
8 slices white bread
chocolate sprinkles
unsweetened (desiccated) coconut
1 pink musk stick, cut into small rounds, or coated candy

S pread butter lightly on bread. Stamp out a mushroom shape with a cutter and sprinkle the stems with chocolate sprinkles and the tops with coconut. Scatter with a few rounds of candy.

Sultana loaf

*The soured milk used in this recipe is made by adding a squeeze of
lemon to whole milk. Serve the loaf sliced and buttered.*

4 oz/125 g self-raising wholemeal (wholewheat) flour
1/4 teaspoon cinnamon
2/3 oz/20 g margarine or softened butter
2 oz/60 g soft brown sugar
2 1/2 oz/75 g sultanas (golden raisins)
1 small egg
3 fl oz/90 ml soured milk

Preheat oven to 350°F (180°C/Gas 4). Grease a 5 1/2 x
3 in (14 x 7.5 cm) loaf pan.

In a large mixing bowl, sift together flour and cinnamon.
Rub through margarine until crumbly. Mix in sugar and
sultanas, and combine well.

In another bowl, whisk egg and milk. Add to dry ingredients and combine well to make a light dough. Spoon into
pan and bake for 25–30 minutes or until a skewer inserted
in the middle comes out clean.

Jigsaw puzzle cake

*For this you will need a large baking tray, about 16 x 13 in
(40 x 33 cm).*

8 oz/250 g butter, softened
6 oz/185 g brown sugar
2 eggs
10 oz/300 g honey
about 1 1/2 lb/750–800 g plain (all-purpose) flour
pinch salt
3 teaspoons ground ginger
2 teaspoons cinnamon
1/2 teaspoon allspice
3 teaspoons bicarbonate of soda (baking soda),
    dissolved in 4 fl oz/125 ml boiling water
royal icing (see recipe opposite), to decorate
food dyes, to decorate

Cream butter and sugar until light and fluffy. Beat in
eggs one at a time, then add honey. Sift together dry
ingredients and add to butter–honey mixture alternately
with dissolved bicarbonate of soda. If the dough feels too
soft, add a little more flour. Shape dough into a ball and
wrap in waxed (greaseproof) paper or plastic wrap.
Refrigerate 2 hours or overnight.

Preheat oven to 325°F (170°C/Gas 3). Cover the back of
a baking tray (about 16 x 13 cin/40 x 30 cm) with non-stick
parchment (baking paper), securing with a little softened
butter. Roll dough out directly onto this tray with a well-
floured rolling pin to a thickness of about 1/4 in (5 mm). Try
to keep it even all over. Trim edges carefully, leaving about
1/2 in (1 cm) around the sides for dough to spread.

Cook for 15 minutes then remove. Using a sharp knife,
cut out large jigsaw shapes—don't be timid, make them
bold and big. Return to oven, reduce heat to 300°F
(150°C/Gas 2), and cook for a further 25–30 minutes.
Remove, and run around the edges of each piece again with
a knife to ensure they are well separated. Let cool, removing
to a wire rack, being careful to keep the puzzle in one shape.

Brush crumbs from individual pieces, then coat each
piece with royal icing (see recipe) using a small spatula to
smooth it over. Reassemble on a large tray and leave the
icing to set, about 2–3 hours or overnight.

When icing is dry, paint a picture on the surface, using
food dyes diluted with water or mixed together for different
shades, and a couple of clean small paint brushes. You may
wish to attempt this task yourself or you may want to ask an
artistic friend to help you. Don't worry too much—after all,
this is a children's birthday party and they will love whatever you do.

Royal icing

This icing can be used for the jigsaw puzzle cake and the face cookies

2 egg whites
1 lb/500 g icing (powdered) sugar, sifted
juice of 1 small lemon

Whisk egg whites until stiff, and gradually beat in
sugar and lemon juice. Keep beating until smooth
and well combined. Keep icing well covered with plastic
wrap to prevent it drying out.

jigsaw puzzle cake

toffee apples

Remove toffee from heat and sit saucepan in a basin of boiling water to prevent it setting. Dip apples quickly into toffee, twirling around for a few seconds, then stand on the baking sheet to set.

Fruit salad ices

1 lb/500 g fruit (e.g. strawberries, bananas, papaya/pawpaw, apple, passionfruit)
juice of 4 oranges
popsicle sticks

*P*repare fruit and cut into small pieces. Combine in a bowl with orange juice, and mix well to combine. Pour mixture into plastic popsicle containers or small paper cups and insert a plastic or wooden stick into the middle of each one. Make sure it sits upright. Freeze overnight. Remove just before serving. To serve, dip the ices in warm water to help release them.

Basket of strawberries birthday cake

There is no need to slave away for hours over a cake that will be demolished in minutes. It's the overall effect that counts with children. Go for something quick and easy to assemble. Some children will want to eat their piece of cake at the table, others can be given a piece to take home.

butter or margarine
plain (all-purpose) flour
9 oz/250 g unsalted butter
8 1/2 oz/240 g caster (superfine) sugar
6 55-g (large) eggs
1 teaspoon vanilla essence/extract
10 1/2 oz/315 g plain (all-purpose) flour
1 1/2 teaspoons baking powder
1 teaspoon bicarbonate of soda (baking soda)
pinch salt
10 fl oz/300 ml sour cream
1 lb/500 g strawberries, washed, dried, and hulled
2 tablespoons sugar

For the buttercream
2 eggs
2 oz/60 g caster (superfine) sugar
6 oz/175 g unsalted butter

Toffee apples

Make these the day before, preferably on a cool dry day. Twirl red ribbon around white plastic sticks for a pretty party look. If any toffee is left over after making the apples, pour it into fancy paper cases and sprinkle with shredded or unsweetened (desiccated) coconut, hundreds and thousands, or vermicelli. If you set the paper cases in patty cake pans, the toffees will hold their shape better while they set.

2 lb/1 kg sugar
20 fl oz/625 ml water
3 fl oz/80 ml vinegar
8 apples
cochineal or red food dye
plastic or wooden sticks

*I*n a heavy saucepan, combine sugar, water, and vinegar, and stir over moderate heat. Continue stirring until all sugar is dissolved. Insert a candy thermometer and boil rapidly until it reaches the hard crack stage 300–310°F (149–154°C). Add a few drops of cochineal to the toffee once it has reached this stage and swirl well to combine. Watch that it doesn't burn.

Meanwhile, wash and polish apples, and push sticks through the cores. Lightly oil a baking sheet.

*P*reheat oven to 350°F (180°C/Gas 4). Butter and flour a 64 fl oz/2 l fluted pan or pudding basin. Cream butter and sugar until light and fluffy. Add eggs one at a time, creaming well after each. If mixture appears to curdle, add 1–2 tablespoons flour and continue adding eggs. Add vanilla. Beat in sifted dry ingredients and sour cream, about one-third at a time, starting and ending with dry ingredients. Pour batter into prepared pan or basin. Smooth the surface. Bake for 60 minutes or until a skewer inserted in the middle comes out clean. Leave cake to settle in pan for 10 minutes, then turn out on a rack to cool completely.

Meanwhile, cut half of the strawberries into dice, sprinkle with sugar, and set aside.

Make buttercream: whisk eggs and sugar until thick and mousse-like, about 10 minutes. In another bowl, cream butter until pale, then add to egg mixture in thirds, creaming well after each addition.

When cake is cold, cut a cone-shaped piece out of the top by inserting a knife at a 45° angle and cutting in a circle. Lift out cone and set aside. Drain diced strawberries through a sieve and reserve juices. Brush inside of cake with reserved strawberry juices. Mix diced strawberries with a third of the buttercream, and spoon into cavity of cake. Set the cut cone upside down on the top to give a mounded effect.

Spread half of leftover buttercream over top of cake. Using a piping bag with a rosette nozzle, decorate top of cake with remaining buttercream. Arrange remaining whole strawberries on top.

fruit salad ices

Games to play

Grandma's Footsteps

Play this game as the children are arriving, as the children can join in at any part of the proceedings. Grandma turns her back and the children try to creep up on her from behind. Every now and again, Grandma will suddenly turn around and if she sees anyone moving they have to go back to the starting point. Anyone, of course, can fill Grandma's role—another helpful adult or one of the children.

Rabbits and Foxes

Ask the children to stand in a circle and hold hands. Put one of the children in the middle to be the rabbit. Ask another child to stand outside the circle and be the fox. The fox tries to catch the rabbit inside the circle, but the other children try to protect the rabbit by raising or lowering their arms to stop the fox from entering the circle.

Beatrix Potter Quiz

Make a list of questions before the party: why did Peter Rabbit get into so much trouble in Mr McGregor's vegetable garden? What was he wearing when he went there? What did his mother give him when she put him to bed? Read the story of Peter Rabbit out aloud at the party, then ask the questions. Any children who know the answer should raise their hands. Keep score of who answered what.

Wizard

One of the children is given a magic wand and with this wand is able to turn the others into anything she or he wishes. The recipient is tapped on the shoulder with the wand and turned into a rabbit, fox, cow, pig, dog, cat or the like, and the children have to act out the role of that particular animal and make the appropriate noises.

Pin the Tail on the Rabbit

Draw a large rabbit onto a piece of cardboard and stick it firmly to a wall. Cut out a tail from another piece of carboard and attach a piece of adhesive (tape, putty, or Blu-tack) so that it will stick. Tie a blindfold around one of the children, spin them around in a circle three or four times, then face the child in the direction of the drawing. Ask the child to stick the tail on the rabbit and write their name next to the attempt. Remove the tail for the next child's turn. Continue until everyone has had a turn.

Hunt for Peter Rabbit's Shoe

Hide a shoe then show the children the matching one so they know what to look for. Whoever finds the missing shoe wins the game.

A buffet

A buffet

Serves 10

Chilled Green Pea Soup

~

**Atlantic Salmon Cutlets with Virgin Olive Oil
and Pink Peppercorns**

Duck Breasts with Green Chartreuse

Asparagus with Capiscum

Polenta with Oyster Mushrooms

~

**Chocolate Torte with Hazlenuts and Praline
served with Berries and
Home-made Honey Icecream**

~

Coffee and Petits Fours

When I was a teenager, we met our boyfriends at buffet parties. They were usually held by the parents of different girls in their homes as a prelude to a dance. Since all the students at my school were girls, this was our only chance to meet boys of the same age in a supervised social setting.

I recall one mother managing to feed 40 people on three chickens because of the amount of white sauce she used ("chicken à la king" was fashionable back then). I admired her thrift, but the white sauce was very bland and even when served with rice, still tended to slop around the plate.

Still, the buffet served its purpose: it fed a reasonably large number of people in an atmosphere of informality that allowed guests to mingle and chat. There are many advantages to this style of entertaining: guests relax and take part in the proceedings when they help pass around the serving dishes, and the buffet itself can be set up in many different ways depending on the season and the amount of space you have. It can be held outdoors or indoors; you can seat people at pre-set tables and chairs if you have room, or they can sit on the floor, the steps, the porch, in the kitchen and even, at times, on the bed. The idea that people usually sit around a table to eat is actually very specific to Western culture.

Setting up

If it's a large crowd, the food can be laid out on one table, and the plates, cutlery, napery, and glasses can be set up on another table or a sideboard (or "buffet", from which this style of entertaining gets its name). If there is enough room around the table, encourage two lines to flow so that things move more quickly. Or try a number of smaller tables: one for plates, one for glasses etc. If it's a smaller crowd, you can place the food at one end of a table and the plates and other items at the other. Make sure there is plenty of room around the table for guests to move, or if there is a shortage of space, push the table up against the wall. You can even set everything out on the tiers of a staircase at waist and shoulder height. Spread each stair with a cloth first, and make it clear to guests that the staircase can't be used as a thoroughfare. The main consideration is that guests should have easy access for serving and "grazing". Whatever set-up you choose, ensure the plates and cutlery for each course are laid out neatly to avoid confusion, and that there are plenty of serving utensils. The plates, one large and one medium-size, should be stacked to a sensible height. The cutlery can be spread out separately, forks in one group, knives in another, perhaps forming a fan. Or offer knives and forks in pairs, caught in a folded napkin such as one in the napkin folding chapter (see page 28). Flowers or candles may be knocked over and are best placed away from the buffet, or at its end.

The presentation

Buffets offer wonderful opportunities to be innovative and creative with the way you present food. The brilliant 19th century French chef and pastrycook Antonin Carême was arguably the most brilliant exponent of the cold buffet, a form of entertainment that dates back to the "credenza" of Renaissance Italy.

Well before Carême's time, the word "buffet" referred to an edifice of shelves erected along one side of the dining hall. In medieval and Renaissance times in France, the family silver was displayed on these, and it was only later, after the Revolution, that food began to be displayed there as well. The idea was to tantalize guests before they sat down to eat. The Italians seem to have been the innovators of the buffet as we know it. Their "credenza"—a course of cold dishes including sausages, pies, shellfish, vegetables, salads, fruits, cakes, and candies—was interspersed with gelatin molds and statues made out of sugar.

Simple food, clever ideas

A buffet at home doesn't need to be anything as grandiose. Do not try to imitate the buffets of five-star hotels and cruise-liners. Keep it simple and beautiful, but make it look as though you have gone to some trouble. Try to think of a focal piece and arrange the other food around it. You could work around a theme: make it Indonesian with a beef rendang and accompaniments such as rice, sambals, chutneys, pappadums, and spicy fruit salad; or perhaps Thai with green chicken curry, jasmine rice, spicy cucumber salad, and a platter of exotic Thai fruits. Or serve lamb kebabs, flat bread and a selection of mezes and salads such as baba ghannouj, hummus with tahini, artichoke hearts in oil, tabbouli, and beetroot and yogurt salad for a Lebanese theme. An Italian theme could involve a seafood salad, chicken pieces roasted with rosemary, garlic, and chili, assorted pasta salads, a rocket salad, a platter of tomatoes, bocconcini, and fresh basil, and zuccotto or zuppa inglese for dessert. Or go Mexican with gazpacho, chicken mole, refried beans, Mexican rice, a stack of tortillas, guacamole and a few other salsas, salad, and a flan or sherbet for dessert.

A buffet should be generous and abundant. Because each guest will generally want to sample each dish, you need to provide more food per person than you would for a formal dinner. But try not to serve too many dishes. People can be overwhelmed by too many choices and end up putting so much food on their plates that individual tastes are lost. When planning your menu, think of how the dishes will work together, both in their tastes and textures and visually. Dishes also quickly end up looking messy and tired when people are serving themselves. If you are serving a large number of guests, replenish platters frequently or have fresh ones in reserve in the kitchen.

The best dishes are made from one or two superb, simple ingredients, prepared well and presented skillfully. In summer, a cold baked ham is a good idea; or a chicken galantine or turkey buffé are also good, but make sure you have a good carver on hand. Vitello tonnato, a cold cooked nut of veal, sliced and filled with tuna mayonnaise, is delicious and practical. Accompanied with different salads (tomato and basil, mixed lettuces, pasta, potato or rice) and an array of pickles, chutneys, mustards, and breads, this is easy and effective entertaining. Try to choose interesting, exotic dishes—they don't have to be expensive.

If you are feeling panicked, which is understandable when catering for large numbers, work out a menu that includes dishes which can be cooked well ahead, frozen, and reheated before the party. Lasagne, moussaka, a spicy curry, or a chicken, bacon, and mushroom pie are all perfect for this situation. And don't spend time and energy cooking high-quality items such as petits fours that can be purchased ready-made from specialty stores. Do all that you can in advance—an absentee host can be unsettling for guests. In the buffet hosted by Katie Highfield which is presented here, all dishes except the fish can be already laid out on the buffet before guests arrive. It is preferable for most food that is not served hot to be at room temperature, rather than chilled from the refrigerator.

Wine suggestions

~ *With the salmon:* a fresh young rosé, preferably from the Loire, Provence or the New World, served well-chilled.

~ *With the duck:* a spicy, medium-weight red, such as a peppery, cool-region Australian shiraz or a Crozes-Hermitage or St Joseph from France's Rhône Valley.

chilled green pea soup

These recipes, which serve 10, can be easily multiplied for 20, 30, or 40 people, but it is wise to try out a recipe first for the smaller quantity. Be judicious when multiplying quantities for salt, pepper, chili powder, and dried herbs. Use less rather than more, and adjust to taste as you proceed.

It is wise not to cook hot dishes for more than about 20 servings in one batch as very large amounts of food take a long time to heat up and to cool. Bacteria thrive under such conditions, especially in chicken dishes. When you re-heat dishes, do so in smallish quantities.

Chilled green pea soup

1¹/2 oz/45 g unsalted butter
2 medium potatoes, peeled and sliced
3 tart green apples, peeled and sliced
2 young white onions, peeled and sliced
6 cups (48 fl oz/1.5 l) chicken stock
1 lb/500 g frozen green peas (not minted)
salt and white pepper
1 cup (8 fl oz/250 ml) crème fraîche

elt butter in a large heavy saucepan. Sauté potatoes, apples, and onion with lid on, until just tender. Add chicken stock. Bring to boil. Remove from heat, add peas, and stir to distribute. Allow to cool.

Blend in batches in food processor or blender until smooth. Season to taste with salt and pepper. Refrigerate, covered, until well chilled.

Serve with a small spoonful of crème fraîche for each serving.

Atlantic salmon cutlets with virgin olive oil and pink peppercorns

This is the only dish you will need to actually cook at the last moment. You may choose to use a char-broiler (grill), barbecue or grill, or a cast-iron grill (broiler) pan which sits on the oven top.

10 Atlantic salmon cutlets about 3/4 in (2 cm) thick
2/3 cup (5 fl oz/160 ml) virgin olive oil
freshly ground black pepper
4 limes, cut in quarters lengthwise
3–4 tablespoons dried pink peppercorns

Place salmon cutlets in a large ceramic or stainless steel flat dish. Pour over olive oil and sprinkle with coarse ground black pepper. Allow to marinate for about 1 hour, turning a few times.

Preheat cooking surface. Cook cutlets 3–4 minutes each side until just crispy on the outside and pink in the middle.

Place on a platter, scatter over pink peppercorns, and arrange lime wedges attractively around fish. Serve immediately.

atlantic salmon cutlets

Heat broiler (grill) until very hot. Place breasts, skin-side down, on the rack. Cook 5–6 in (13–15 cm) from the heat for about 5 minutes. Turn breasts over and cook until skin is golden. Remove from heat and allow to rest.

Combine remaining Chartreuse, orange juice, and marmalade in a small saucepan. Bring to a boil, then simmer 2–3 minutes or until syrupy.

Slice duck breasts, arrange on platter, and then spoon over the glaze. Garnish with orange zest.

Asparagus with capsicum

5 bunches green asparagus, with 2 in (5 cm) trimmed from
  bottom of stalks
6 large red capsicums (bell peppers), stalk ends, seeds,
  and membranes removed
4 fl oz/125 ml virgin olive oil
1 teaspoon flaky sea salt
freshly ground black pepper
zest of 2 lemons

Drop asparagus spears into a pan of rapidly boiling salted water and cook for 2-3 minutes until they turn dark green and become tender. Pat dry and set aside.

Preheat oven to 400°F (200°C/Gas 6).

Place capsicums on a lightly oiled piece of foil on a baking sheet, leaving some space between each. Bake for 25-30 minutes until blistered and blackened. Alternatively, place the tray under a hot grill (broiler). After cooking, place capsicums in a plastic bag to sweat. When cool enough to handle, remove from bag and peel off skin with your fingers. Slice into wide strips.

Arrange asparagus and capsicum on a serving platter. Drizzle with oil, sprinkle with sea salt and pepper, and scatter with lemon zest. Serve at room temperature.

Polenta with oyster mushrooms

This recipe comes from Diane Holuigue's Master Class.

For the polenta
24 fl oz/750 ml chicken stock
8 oz/250 g polenta
1 teaspoon salt
freshly ground black pepper
2 oz/60 g unsalted butter
3 tablespoons freshly grated parmesan
1 tablespoon chopped fresh thyme, optional
virgin olive oil

duck breasts with green Chartreuse

Duck breasts with green Chartreuse

This recipe will amply serve 10 people or more.

10 boned duck breasts
2 fl oz/60 ml olive oil
freshly ground black pepper
6 fl oz/180 ml green Chartreuse
3 fl oz/80 ml freshly squeezed orange juice
3 fl oz/80 ml thinly shredded lime marmalade
zest of 1 orange

Place duck breasts in a large ceramic or stainless steel flat dish. Rub with olive oil and pepper, and pour over half the Chartreuse. Allow to marinate 1–2 hours or overnight, turning from time to time.

polenta with oyster mushrooms

For the mushrooms
4 tablespoons olive oil
1¹/₂ lb/750 g oyster mushrooms
2 tablespoons chopped fresh thyme
flaky sea salt
freshly ground black pepper

*P*lace chicken stock into a large saucepan and bring to boil. Add polenta, and stir vigorously, using a strong wire whisk to prevent lumps from forming. Add salt and pepper and continue to whisk for about 10 minutes. When polenta has become quite stiff, stir in butter, parmesan, and thyme.

Spread polenta into a buttered baking dish, about 8 in x 8 in (20 x 20 cm). Press down with your fingers. Let cool until firm and ready to serve.

Cut polenta into serving squares or triangles. Brush each piece with olive oil on both sides and season with salt and pepper. When ready, cook under a hot grill (broiler) for about 5 minutes or until golden.

Meanwhile, heat 4 tablespoons oil in a large heavy-based frying pan. Toss in mushrooms, thyme, salt, and a good grinding of pepper. Turn mushrooms with a wooden spoon until just cooked.

To serve, arrange warm polenta on a platter and spoon mushrooms over.

Chocolate torte with hazelnuts and praline

Serve with honey icecream (see recipe) and fresh berries in season

For the torte

4 oz/125 g unsalted butter, roughly chopped
8 oz/250 g unsweetened (bitter cooking) chocolate, roughly chopped
8 egg yolks
8 oz/250 g caster (superfine) sugar
6 oz/185 g roasted hazelnuts, skinned and finely chopped
5 egg whites

For the praline

8 oz/250 g lightly toasted blanched almonds, roughly chopped
14 oz/400 g caster (superfine) sugar
4 fl oz/125 ml water

Preheat oven to 350°F (180°C/Gas 4). Lightly butter and flour a 10-in (25-cm) springform pan.

Melt butter and chocolate together in a microwave oven or in a bowl over steaming water. Stir well to combine. Whisk together egg yolks and sugar until thick and creamy. Fold chocolate mixture into the egg mixture, then fold in hazelnuts. Stir to combine. Whisk egg whites in another bowl until stiff. Fold a spoonful through the chocolate–nut mixture to lighten, then fold through remaining whites lightly until well combined. Pour mixture into pan.

Bake 30–35 minutes or until a skewer inserted in the middle comes out clean. Remove from oven and set on a wire rack to cool. When cool, remove springform.

Meanwhile, lightly oil a baking sheet and sprinkle with almonds. In a heavy-based saucepan, bring sugar and water to a boil, stirring until sugar has dissolved. Simmer until syrup looks like caramel. Pour syrup over nuts. Let cool.

Break praline into pieces, and process in food processor until medium fine. Scatter over the cake.

opposite: chocolate torte with hazelnuts and praline, honey icecream

Honey icecream

Use a full-bodied honey for best results—leatherwood is good, or you can try lavender or mimosa.

10 egg yolks
12 oz/375 g good-quality honey
4 cups (32 fl oz/1 l) milk
8 fl oz/250 ml thickened or whipping cream
8 fl oz/250 ml crème fraîche

Beat egg yolks and honey together until light and creamy. Bring milk to a boil in a saucepan. Pour slowly over egg yolk mixture, whisking constantly. Pour into a heavy-based saucepan and stir over low heat until mixture thickens and coats the back of a wooden spoon. Remove from heat and let cool. Refrigerate for 1–2 hours or overnight.

Fold in cream and crème fraîche, and process in an ice-cream machine for best results. (If you don't have one: freeze mixture, then beat with fork, then re-freeze and re-beat 3 times at 20 minute intervals.)

Cocktail parties for six or sixty

Cocktail parties for six or sixty

Herbed Focaccia

Crudités with Red Capsicum Dip

Pastries
Creamed Gorgonzola ~ Mixed Mushroom

Crab-Filled Egg Rolls

Lemongrass and Ginger Mussels

Star Octopus on Crostini with Aioli

Sashimi Tuna on Cucumber Rounds

Ribbon Sandwiches

Cocktails
Berry Punch ~ White Sangría ~ Margarita

*W*hen I think of cocktail parties, the images that spring to mind are straight out of the 1930s. Men in dinner jackets, women in straight, low-waisted dresses and long beads with bandeaux wrapped around their foreheads, impeccable waiters in black ties and starched white shirts, silver cocktail shakers and an endless stream of martinis...

I have to confess that this fantasy far outstrips the reality of the cocktail parties I actually do hold. But you don't have to be a Great Gatsby—an informal gathering where guests can kick up their heels and have a good time serves a number of purposes in your entertaining diary.

Cocktail parties lend themselves to many interpretations. They can be as large or small as you wish, and as formal or informal as you choose. When you are busy working all week and can't find the time to prepare and cook for a dinner party, a small cocktail party for six to eight people can be a way of catching up before you go on to a show or out to a restaurant.

No matter what type of cocktail party you throw, however, it should comprise both drinks and food. If you offer drinks only, your guests may really start to feel the effects (and side effects) of alcohol and the omission of food becomes rather irresponsible. Indeed, the dictionary definition of "cocktail" is that it is both a drink and an appetizer. Some say the word derives from cutting the tail of any horse that wasn't a thoroughbred, so that by definition a "cocktail" was a mixture. Others believe it derived from the tail of the cockerel which "cocks up" and to the cock fights, wherein the birds were given an alcoholic concoction to improve their chances of winning. Whatever its derivations, cocktails came into their own during the prohibition era of the 1920s and 1930s, when mixed drinks were the only way to make bootleg alcohol acceptable.

Hosting a party

Cocktail parties are a great way to entertain a lot of people at one time and of introducing new people into your social spectrum. Perhaps such guests aren't necessarily those you'd feel comfortable inviting (yet) to a more intimate event such as a dinner party.

Granted this, they offer excellent occasions, as the host, to make and maintain contact with others; and as a guest, to meet those not normally encountered in the usual round of social activities. It's a good opportunity to "mix 'n match" people and take a few risks: you might invite the person who has just moved in next door, for example, or an eccentric cousin. Often the more eclectic the combination, the livelier the party. You don't have to worry so much about compatibility as the time is short and the guests mobile.

People stand and move about in fairly close contact with one another, glass in one hand, and help themselves to the food on offer. This mobility should be encouraged for often cocktail parties are about meeting as many people as possible. As host, it's your role to make sure people move about and meet others. Keep an eye on guests who tend to be shy by nature—don't let them get stuck against a wall with another shy or a very domineering person, and try to discourage small "exclusive" clusters. More gregarious types will need no help in "working the room", but they too may occasionally need supervising if their attention-seeking ways get out of hand, and that is your responsibility as host.

There are a few guidelines for holding a successful cocktail party. How many people you invite will depend on how much space you have. Work out how many people your living spaces will fit comfortably, and move furniture around—or out—to suit. Many people these days are happy for a cocktail party to spill over into their kitchen. A small room filled with too many people is both uncomfortable and claustrophobic. There's nothing worse than feeling you can't breathe or that someone else's drink is inadvertently trickling down your back. A "cosy" crowd is what you should aim for. On the other hand, if the space is too large, people might float around feeling a bit lost and the vitality of the party will be sapped. If you'd like people to dance, you'll need to provide suitable music (jazz is perfect for a cocktail party) and a room that has been cleared of furniture.

The hours you specify on your invitation will determine the type of party you hold. If the hours are 5-7 pm or 6-8 pm, it signals a party that is a prelude to dinner or to some other function. Platters of different finger foods will be perfect provisions for your guests. If the hours are 6-9 pm, 7-10 pm, or later, you will need to provide something more substantial, along the lines of a mini-buffet. And children? You will need to establish if their presence is appropriate, and this depends on their age: young teenagers can be very helpful behind a bar, especially if briefed well and even paid for their efforts, whereas toddlers will need constant supervision.

You will also need to decide if you need—and can afford—help. At a larger gathering of 40-60 people, one or two hired helpers can make a huge difference. They can help replenish drinks, clear away glasses and pass around platters of food. A professional cocktail bartender is another consideration— watching the making and shaking of drinks will help focus the party, lending an air of theatricality to the event, and the expertise will ensure that a wide variety of cocktails can be offered.

Finger food

There's nothing worse than a flustered host or guest. And there's nothing more unwieldy or irritating than food in the hand that is dripping or needs cutting. When thinking of the food for a cocktail party, think simple and bite-size. Provide small plates and napkins, and make sure to provide small bowls for toothpicks and the like.

In general, aim for food that is neither dry nor crumbly, sticky nor fatty. Sogginess must be avoided. Freshness is all-important—crunch and texture on the crudité platter; wispy light pastry cases and crisp crostini. Try to strike a balance between cold platters and those offering hot food (though the latter require more time in the kitchen), and to mix in a few substantial items (such as sandwiches) with lighter ones. Use your judgment regarding the number of dishes served and the quantities. As a rule, allow 12-15 pieces of cocktail food per person and a choice of about 6 different items for a 2-3 hour party.

Wine suggestions

~ With the crudités: a chilled, fresh, fino Sherry.

~ With the mussels: a very young, tangy racy dry white such as a sauvignon blanc from New Zealand's Marlborough region.

~ With the sandwiches: sparkling wine, preferably a premium bottled-fermented sparkling variety from Australia or California.

Herbed focaccia

These can be made well ahead and frozen, then defrosted and cut into "fingers" or triangles. They are nice served on their own or with a dab of goat's cheese. Set aside some time to make them as they require a few hours to prove (see glossary).

2 lb/1 kg plain (all-purpose) unbleached flour
1 sachet (7g–1/4 oz) dry yeast
1 tablespoon flaky sea salt
21 fl oz/625 ml warm water
2 tablespoons olive oil
extra 1 oz/30 ml warm water, if required

For green olive and sage focaccia
18 large green olives, pits (stones) removed and flesh chopped
12–15 large sage leaves, finely shredded
flaky sea salt

For the rosemary focaccia
leaves from 2 stalks fresh rosemary, chopped
1 finely chopped red chili, seeded, optional

For tops
flaky sea salt
mixture of half water and half oil
extra sage leaves
extra rosemary leaves

*I*n a large mixing bowl combine flour with yeast and salt. Make a hole in the middle and add warm water and olive oil. Combine to make a dough, adding a little extra water if needed. Transfer to a floured bench and knead for about 10 minutes or until smooth and elastic. If sticky, work in a little more flour. Alternatively, use an electric mixer with a dough hook: knead the dough at low speed for 2 minutes, then for a further 4–5 minutes, or until dough is smooth and elastic.

Place dough into a lightly oiled large bowl and cover with oiled plastic wrap and a cloth. Let stand in a warm place for 1 1/2 hours or until doubled in bulk (length of time will depend on temperature of the day). Transfer to a floured bench, knock down (see glossary), and divide into two equal portions.

For the green olive and sage focaccia, knead olives and sage through one half of the dough, continuing to knead until well incorporated. For the rosemary focaccia, knead rosemary and chili through the dough, continuing to knead until well incorporated. Roll both portions out with a lightly floured rolling pin to fit 2 oiled baking sheets (about 9 x 11 in/23 x 28 cm). Place on sheets, flattening with the palms of your hands and pushing dough out to edges. Let stand 30 minutes.

Dimple tops of focaccia with your fingers, and sprinkle each one with flaky sea salt. Scatter extra sage leaves on green olive and sage focaccia, and sprinkle lightly with a mixture of olive oil and water. Repeat with the rosemary focaccia, sprinkling top with extra rosemary leaves. Let stand another 30 minutes.

Preheat oven to 400°F (200°C/Gas 6). Bake 20–25 minutes, spraying with water a few times during the first 10 minutes (use an atomizer or brush on). Turn out onto racks to cool.

herbed focaccia

Crudités

Choose interesting vegetables in season: baby carrots, tiny yellow squash, strips of capsicums (bell peppers) in different shades, tiny yellow tear-drop tomatoes, white and red Belgian endive (chicory), snow peas (mange-touts), and golden mushrooms (enoki) are just some ideas. As a general rule, allow about 5–6 pieces per person.

Some vegetables can be blanched quickly in rapidly boiling salted water and refreshed under cold water. This helps to bring out the taste. Vegetables which profit from this method of preparation include cauliflower, broccoli, asparagus, green beans, baby carrots, squash, and sugar snap peas. Some (for example, green beans) require only 1 minute, others (for example, broccoli and cauliflower) 3–4 minutes. Do not overcook—the vegetables should be crunchy. Dry well after draining and store in separate sealed containers in the refrigerator. Prepare only a few hours ahead; if left overnight, they lose their freshness.

For vegetables which are served fresh, not blanched, use your imagination as to how to cut and present them. Tear-drop tomatoes can be left whole or sliced in half lengthwise; tiny squash can be left whole or sliced into halves or quarters.

If using quail eggs, they can be boiled the day before and sliced in half just before serving.

Use your imagination, too, for containers for dips—a seeded capsicum (bell pepper) makes an ideal container, that is sturdy but decorative.

Serve the crudités with one or more dips. You can use aioli (see recipe, page 166) or any of those listed in our Barbecue menu (see page 53). The red capsicum dip (below) is pungent, offsetting the vegetables well.

Red capsicum dip

Makes about 32 fl oz/1 l

5 red capsicums (bell peppers), halved, seeded and
 membranes removed
1 large potato, peeled and cubed
1 red chili, seeds and stems removed
2 cloves garlic, crushed
1 teaspoon sea salt
3¹/2 fl oz/100 ml olive oil

Cook capsicums, skin-side up, under a hot grill (broiler) until skin is blistered and black. Place in a plastic bag, and seal the top, to sweat. When cool enough to handle, peel skin off with fingers.

Cook potato until soft in boiling salted water. Drain.

Process capsicum, chili, garlic, salt, and potato in a food processor until well combined, then drizzle in oil. Refrigerate until ready to serve.

crudités, red capsicum dip

Preheat oven to 400°F (200°C/Gas 6). To ensure pastry stays fine and in shape, you can either lightly prick each pastry shell with a fork and line with foil or non-stick baking paper (parchment) weighed down with a handful of dry beans. Alternatively, put another patty-pan tray on top and press down firmly to form perfectly shaped pie crusts.

Bake 6–7 minutes or until edges start to darken slightly, then remove weights or pans, and return to oven to dry out for a further 5–7 minutes. Do not brown. Remove to racks to cool.

Fillings

As well as the fillings suggested below, try other simple but delicious fillings, such as lightly scrambled egg topped with salmon roe and snipped chives; crème fraîche or sour cream topped with red or black lumpfish roe; or smoked salmon, curled decoratively over a spoonful of sour cream, and garnished with capers and a thin slice of onion.

Creamed gorgonzola

Fills 24 pastry cases

8 oz/250 g ricotta
3 1/2 oz/100 g gorgonzola
freshly ground black pepper
1 red apple, skin left on, thinly slivered
1 green apple, skin left on, thinly slivered
juice of 1 lemon

*I*n a small mixing bowl, combine ricotta and gorgonzola with a fork. Add pepper and mix well. Spoon into prepared pastry cases. Top with slivers of apple dipped in lemon juice to prevent staining.

Mixed mushroom

Fills 12 pastry cases

Use a mixture of button, oyster (shimeji), and golden (enoki) mushrooms when making these delicate tarts.

5 oz/150 g mixed mushrooms
2 tablespoons olive oil
1 clove garlic, crushed
1 tablespoon snipped chives
salt and pepper

*T*hinly slice button mushrooms. If large, halve or quarter the oyster mushrooms, as they need to sit daintily inside the pastry cases. Trim some of the stems from the enoki if they are too long.

*pastry cases with creamed gorgonzola
and mixed mushroom fillings*

Pastry cases

Makes 36–40 pastry cases
Make these pastry cases well ahead and freeze in freezer bags or plastic containers. If you don't have a food processor, follow the method for making pastry outlined in the recipe for mince pies on page 186.

7 oz/200 g plain (all-purpose) flour
1/2 teaspoon salt
3 1/2 oz/100 g cold unsalted butter, chopped roughly
1 egg yolk
3–4 tablespoons cold water

*S*ift flour and salt into bowl of food processor. Add butter, and process until mixture resembles breadcrumbs. Add egg yolk and water, and process until dough forms a ball around blades. Remove, wrap in waxed (greaseproof) paper, and let rest in refrigerator for 1 hour.

Divide pastry into thirds. Work with one-third at a time, returning the other two to the refrigerator. Lightly dust each third with flour, and roll out thinly between sheets of plastic wrap. Cut into rounds with a cutter, and line 12 2 1/2-in (6-cm) diameter greased patty pans. Chill again. Repeat with remaining pastry.

Heat oil in a frying pan and add garlic. Sauté 1 minute, then add mushrooms. Cook, stirring frequently, until softened. Remove from heat, sprinkle with chives, and season with salt and pepper. Pile into warmed pastry cases and serve warm.

Crab-filled egg rolls

Makes 30 rolls

The nori (seaweed) can be bought from Asian specialty stores.

10 oz/300 g canned crab meat, well-drained
2 tablespoons chopped coriander leaves (cilantro)
salt and pepper
squeeze of fresh lemon juice
6 large eggs
1 tablespoon water
1 teaspoon soy sauce
1 teaspoon fish sauce
few drops vegetable oil
3 sheets nori (seaweed)

*L*ine a baking sheet with plastic wrap. In a bowl, mix crab meat and coriander, seasoning to taste with salt, pepper, and lemon juice. Set aside.

In another bowl, whisk together eggs, water, soy sauce, and fish sauce.

Heat a few drops oil in an 8-in (20-cm) diameter non-stick frying pan, and pour in 1½ fl oz (40 ml) of egg mixture to make a crêpe. Tilt pan while pouring so that it is lightly covered with egg mixture. Cook 1 minute, then flip, and cook a further minute on the other side. Turn out onto the plastic-lined baking sheet. Cook another two crêpes and turn out on top of the first (you need a stack of three crêpes for each roll).

Cut nori into a circle the same size as crêpes, and place one sheet on top of each stack of three crêpes. Divide crab mixture into three and place one-third mixture across bottom end of each nori/crêpe stack. Roll up tightly, using plastic to secure the roll (only one stack should be on the plastic each time). Refrigerate rolls for ½ hour, then cut each one into 10 slices. Arrange decoratively on a platter.

crab-filled egg rolls

Discard any mussels with broken shells. Bring wine and water to a boil in a large frying pan. Add a layer of mussels, and remove with a slotted spoon or tongs as they open. Continue adding more as cooked ones are removed. Discard any that do not open. Let cool a little, remove top shell of each mussel, and discard.

For the dressing: Pound lemongrass with a mallet until flat and pliable. Chop finely and put into a mixing bowl. Finely chop coriander root and halfway up the stems (reserving leaves for garnish). Add to the mixing bowl along with chili, sesame oil, ginger, lemon juice, and vegetable oil. Season with salt to taste, and add more lemon juice if desired.

Spoon a little dressing over each mussel and serve on a platter in their shells, garnished with reserved coriander leaves. Store in refrigerator, covered with plastic wrap.

Star octopus on crostini with aioli

Makes 30

A good fishmonger will sort the tiny octopus out for you from the rest. Otherwise, go to a fishmarket and sort through the small octopus, choosing the tiniest ones available.

30 tiny octopus
1/2 carrot
1 celery stalk
1/2 onion
bay leaf
few peppercorns
juice of 1 lemon
1–2 ficelles (thin French bread sticks), cut on the diagonal
    into 30 slices

For the aioli
3 egg yolks, at room temperature
2 cloves garlic, crushed
1 3/4 fl oz/50 ml white wine vinegar
1/2 teaspoon sea salt
14 fl oz/400 ml olive oil

1 bunch chives, for garnish

To prepare octopus, hold the head of each firmly and cut through the flesh below the eyes. Discard head, as you need only the tentacles for these bite-size pieces. Pick up the tentacles and, with the index finger underneath, gently push out the beak or mouth, and discard.

lemongrass and ginger mussels

Lemongrass and ginger mussels

Makes about 30
These mussels can be served at room temperature or cold.

2 lb/1 kg unshelled mussels, scrubbed and bearded
8 fl oz/250 ml dry white wine
8 fl oz/250 ml water

For the dressing
1 stalk lemongrass
2 stalks fresh coriander (cilantro), root attached
1 small hot chili, stem removed, seeded, and finely chopped
2 tablespoons sesame oil
1 tablespoon finely chopped fresh ginger
juice of 1–2 lemons
3 1/2 fl oz/100 ml vegetable oil
salt

star octopus on crostini with aioli

Place octopus in a saucepan and cover with water. Add carrot, celery, onion, bay leaf, and peppercorns. Bring to a boil, skimming off any scum, then turn off immediately. Let octopus sit in water for 2–3 minutes, then check to see if they are cooked: they will still be quite firm, but the point of a sharp knife should pierce through the middle easily. Remove with a slotted spoon to dry on paper towels. They should look like tiny stars. Wipe perfectly clean, squeeze a little lemon juice over each one, and store, covered, in refrigerator.

To make crostini: preheat oven to 400°F (200°C/Gas 6). Place bread-stick slices in one layer on a baking sheet, and toast in oven for 5–10 minutes until crisp and golden. When cool, store in an airtight container.

To make aioli: process egg yolks, garlic, vinegar, and salt in a blender or food processor until combined, then add oil, drop by drop at first and then in a fine stream, until mixture is thick and creamy.

To assemble, put a generous spoonful of aioli onto each crostini. Top with prepared octopus. Place elegantly on a platter lined with a spray of chives.

sashimi tuna on cucumber rounds

Sashimi tuna on cucumber rounds

Ask your fishmonger to slice the tuna for you. You will only need tiny pieces as they have to sit comfortably curled up on a round of cucumber. Be careful: the wasabi is strong.

wasabi (green horseradish) paste
1 telegraph (continental) cucumber, sliced into 30 rounds
  about 1/4 in (5 mm) thick
30 tiny slices pickled pink ginger, dried
30 small slices sashimi tuna
black sesame seeds
fresh coriander leaves (cilantro), for garnish

Place a small dab of wasabi paste onto each cucumber slice. Entwine each piece of ginger with a piece of tuna, and place on cucumber slice, pressing on to the wasabi paste to hold. Sprinkle with black sesame seeds. Garnish each slice with a leaf of coriander.

Ribbon sandwiches

Instructions for making these sandwiches are in the Afternoon Tea menu (see page 89). Use different fillings: try roast beef and mustard, tuna mayonnaise, or egg and watercress.

Cocktails

Try not to serve too many cocktails unless you have employed a professional cocktail bartender; otherwise you'll spend all night behind the bar mixing and shaking, and not be able to play the role of host. Limit the number of types of cocktails to two or three—perhaps a martini and a margarita. Ready-mixed cocktails will help minimize work.

A large mixed drink, such as a punch or sangria (see recipes below), is a good idea, as it can be made ahead and guests can help themselves.

Champagne is always welcome. Other drinks such as gin and tonic, scotch on the rocks, white rum and cola, and dry vermouth may also be served.

Be specific about what you have to offer: when guests arrive, give them a guideline by offering a selection of two or three that you have chosen. If you ask "What would you like to drink?", your guest is in the awkward position of having to guess what might or might not be available.

If you don't have a bar, set one up on a table. If you put a sheet of glass or plastic cloth over it, it will protect the table and make it easier to wipe. An ice bucket is important, though a bathtub comes in handy. Drinks can be kept cold if interspersed between bags of ice in the tub. A cocktail shaker is essential if making shaken cocktails, and an ice hammer and tongs also come in handy. A strainer and a long-handled spoon are also useful for cocktails. A juice squeezer and electric blender will be essential if making fruit-based drinks.

Make sure there are plenty of cloth towels handy and a bottle opener. And lots of pre-cut orange and lemon slices are good for garnishing drinks. Check your glasses: champagne flutes, short and tall tumblers, and V-shaped cocktail glasses. You may need to hire extra for the evening. Before using, wipe out with a clean cloth to ensure they are sparkling.

Margarita

This is a Mexican cocktail which has become internationally popular. Prepare the glasses beforehand by dipping the rim of each glass into lime juice and then into a plate of fine salt—this frosts the rim. Store the glasses in the refrigerator if you have the space. This recipe is for a quantity per person.

1 fl oz/30 ml tequila
1 fl oz/30 ml Cointreau
1 fl oz/30 ml freshly squeezed lime juice
1 cup crushed ice

Pour the tequila, Cointreau, and lime juice into a cocktail shaker with ice. Shake well, strain, and pour into the prepared glasses.

ribbon sandwiches

Berry punch

This is good for a large cocktail party. The following measures are per person and the quantities should be multiplied by the number of people you want to serve. A handy tip to keep a large quantity of punch chilled is to use a big block of ice in the bowl, as it won't melt as quickly as ice cubes. Make sure the drinks are cold before mixing.

2 fl oz/60 ml champagne/sparkling wine
2 fl oz/60 ml lemonade (e.g 7–UP, Sprite)
1 fl oz/30 ml strawberry midori
¹/2 fl oz/15 ml vodka
juice of ¹/2 lemon, or to taste
2 oz/60 g fresh or frozen whole berries (e.g. strawberries, blueberries, blackcurrant, raspberries)

*P*lace all ingredients, except berries, in a jug or punch bowl. Stir well to combine. Adjust for sweetness/sourness by adding more lemonade or lemon juice. Stir in berries and pour into glasses over ice cubes.

White sangría

Serves 10

This is a fresh alternative to the berry punch. If you are serving it in summer, float borage flowers on the top and garnish with pineapple mint or spearmint and a few sliced strawberries.

2 24-fl oz/750-ml bottles dry white wine
2 tablespoons brandy
2 oranges, thinly sliced
1 lemon or lime, thinly sliced
juice of 2 oranges
3–4 tablespoons caster (superfine) sugar
crushed ice

*P*our wine and brandy into a large jug or glass bowl. Add citrus fruits and juices. Stir in sugar and add more to taste if desired. Chill well for about 2 hours in the refrigerator, then serve in glasses over crushed ice.

berry punch

A festive Christmas

A festive Christmas

Serves 10-14

Grand Marnier Pâté

Oysters

~

Leg of Ham

**Roast Turkey with
Pork and Veal Forcemeat & Fruit and Nut Stuffing
Served with Roasted Vegetables**

Candied Sweet Potatoes

Green Beans

Brussels Sprouts and Chestnuts

Gravy

Cranberry Sauce

~

**Royal Christmas Pudding
Served with Custard and/or Hard Sauce**

Millie Sherman's Christmas Cake with White Icing

~

Mince Pies

Gingerbread Men

Christmas Trees

*t*he boxes are lifted down and sorted in late November. The past year's dust is brushed off, accompanied by much sneezing, and the wreath and decorations lifted out. The ribbons are pressed. Almost overnight the house is transformed.

So begins another Christmas. My mother actually prepares for Chrismas all year. She goes to sales, buys gifts and stores them away in cupboards. An idle moment might catch her pushing cloves into oranges, embroidering a nightgown for a grand-daughter, topping up the fruit mince with brandy or, come October, shopping for the fruit and nuts for the cake and plum pudding.

All families have their own traditions and ours is no exception. My mother has always acknowledged the magical quality of the occasion and sees it as a change of pace from the normal daily routine of our lives. Christmas is celebrated at my parents' house; we gather there from far and wide, and because my mother is so enraptured with the idea of Christmas in the Anglo Saxon-style, that is how we celebrate.

During the second week of December, my father purchases the tree. The moment he carries it inside, the smell of the pine needles fills the house; that glorious smell, so evocative of Christmas. Apparently, it was Prince Albert who introduced the custom to England by transporting cut conifers from Germany in the 19th century. My daughter decorates the tree, having claimed this as her job over the years.

When we were younger and still living at home, my parents invited friends to visit on Christmas Eve. Outside, the garden statues were decorated with red bows and a sprig or two of holly, and the trees strewn with fairy lights. Inside, the bannisters were tied with bows, mirrors hung with garlands of flowers, and gingerbread men, Christmas cookies, oranges, nuts, and dried fruit were set in bowls throughout the house. In the dining room, a table groaned with food. On the table in the front hall, a gingerbread house sat, waiting to be demolished by little hands and mouths at the end of the evening. For that was the night on which spirits were high and we children full of anticipation and excitement. We would spend weeks preparing for this party, baking cookies, creating papier mâché ornaments to hang on the tree, and making and wrapping gifts to give to friends.

These days, it is our children who fill the house with Christmas spirit, and our main celebration—after the frenzied opening of presents under the tree on Christmas morning—is either a mid-afternoon lunch or an early dinner on the day. We usually eat a good breakfast of thick slices of ham with fried eggs and buttered toast accompanied by champagne and orange juice so our appetites are appeased until early afternoon.

On the days before Christmas...

A successful Christmas meal is dependent on careful timing, and its preparation is an important part of the Christmas day ritual. The reason my family leave our feast until later in the day is so we have time to set the table, prepare and cook the turkey, vegetables, and crème anglaise. If you prepare as much as possible ahead, there should be no reason to panic on the day.

Make the plum pudding up to six months ahead, and the mincemeat and Christmas cake two to three months ahead. They will mature, becoming richer and darker, and you won't have to worry about them at the last moment. The plum pudding will need extra steaming on the day, so make sure you allow room on your stove for that.

A feast such as this calls for out-of-the-ordinary ingredients, so you will have to plan your shopping. Order the turkey four to six weeks ahead (perhaps a ham as well if

catering for a crowd); order your champagne and wine then too. The brandy butter can be made a couple of weeks ahead and stored in a sealed container in the refrigerator. The gingerbread men, mince pies, and pâté can be made a few days in advance. You can even set the table then too if you won't have to use it before the meal. Make sure the silver is polished and the placemats and napkins clean and starched. Check your cutlery and glasses and put together your floral arrangements. Bunches of holly are perfect tied with red bows and will last for weeks. The day before is time to prepare the stuffing, and make the stock and the toast for the pâté.

For me, these are the ingredients of a perfect Christmas because it is my Christmas and that of my family. Familiarity is an important part of the season and there is something very special about sharing the Christmas meal with those you love—be it friends or family. Bringing your own ideas to the existing traditions will add your personal stamp to the occasion and contribute to your own special memories of Christmas.

The dinner

A selection of festive food—such as the Christmas cake and the mince pies—should be presented on a sideboard, buffet, or table so that people can help themselves throughout the day or evening.

Begin the meal with the pâté, followed by the oysters, letting the guests choose how many they would like. Then, the highlight of the meal, bring out the turkey on a large platter surrounded by the roast vegetables. Serve the other vegetables on separate platters for people to help themselves. Pass around the cranberry jelly and the gravy boat (make sure to warm the boat first by rinsing with boiling water and drying before pouring in the gravy).

Deck the halls

~ *It really makes a difference if effort is put into decorating the table. Bonbons lend a festive air— allow one per person at each setting. Lighting helps set the mood—gold candles in antique hurricane lamps are just one option. Your decorations may be limited by the space available on the table, but if you have room, enliven the middle of your table with holly tied with red bows. Fresh flowers are also a lovely addition. Try to use red, green, and orange to continue the Christmas theme.*

~ *Sprinkle a drop of perfume (perhaps essential oil of frankincense or myrrh) on the light bulbs throughout the house to fill the rooms with a wonderful aroma.*

~ *Fill bowls with oranges or apples for bright but simple decoration. Pomanders of oranges studded with cloves will bring a heady aroma to a room.*

~ *Pine cones and bundles of cinnamon sticks tied together are a nice touch anywhere in the house.*

~ *Using white, green, and red origami paper, make origami birds to hang in the tree.*

~ *As well as those made for eating, bake extra gingerbread men, trees, and stars (leaving a hole at the top) to hang from the Christmas tree.*

~ *Make a wreath with prunings from vines and climbers that have been soaked in the bathtub. Shape into a tight, even circle or loosely formed one, according to your fancy. Then entwine it with ribbons, holly, and baubles.*

~ *Be adventurous. Bring in a garden statue and adorn it with holly for a fun touch.*

~ *Music can really bring the season alive for young and old alike. Try playing Bach's Oratorio, Handel's Messiah, and Nat King Cole's Christmas carols.*

Grand Marnier pâté

The pâté can be prepared a few days ahead, sealed, and left covered with plastic wrap in the refrigerator.

8 fl oz/250 ml dry white wine
1 lb/500 g chicken livers, trimmed of sinew
6¹/2 oz/200 g unsalted butter, softened
3 tablespoons Grand Marnier or other orange liqueur
1–2 teaspoons finely grated orange zest
salt and pepper
pinch allspice
fine strips of orange zest, for decoration
¹/4 teaspoon peppercorns
3 oz/90 g clarified butter, melted, for sealing
1 loaf bread

Bring wine to a boil in a saucepan, add chicken livers, and bring back to a boil. Let simmer for exactly 3 minutes, drain, and cool.

Process livers in a food processor, adding butter knob by knob. Add Grand Marnier and orange zest, and season with salt, pepper, and allspice. Taste for seasoning and orange zest—you should be able to taste the orange. If you prefer a very fine pâté, pass it through a sieve at this stage.

Spoon the mixture into a pretty Christmas dish or bowl, and smooth the surface with a spatula. Decorate the top with strips of orange peel and peppercorns. Let melted butter cool a little and pour carefully over the top. Let butter solidify then refrigerate.

Serve with thin whispers of toast, made by slicing bread very finely and toasting in a moderate oven or under a grill (broiler) until pale gold.

Oysters

5–7 dozen oysters (allow ¹/2 dozen per person)
crushed ice
lime or lemon wedges

Set oysters out on a platter which has been lined with crushed ice. Serve with lime or lemon wedges.

Grand Marnier pâté

oysters

Roast turkey

Turkeys were introduced into Spain by the Jesuits after Columbus discovered the Americas and have taken pride of place on the English Christmas table since the 17th century. It has become traditional to fill the turkey with two stuffings—one for the neck or crop (in this case, pork and veal) and another for the body (fruit and walnut).

1 turkey, 12 lb/6 kg
1 quantity pork and veal forcemeat (see recipe opposite)
1 quantity fruit and nut stuffing (see recipe opposite)
2^1/2 oz/75 g butter, softened
cinnamon
salt and freshly ground pepper

Preheat oven to 220°F (425°C/Gas 7). Wipe turkey dry both inside and out with paper towels. Put pork and veal forcemeat into the neck. Be careful not to pack it in too tightly as it will swell as it cooks. Pull neck skin over the cavity and secure with skewers.

Put fruit and nut stuffing into body of the turkey. Tuck wings underneath and plump up breasts to give it a good shape. Pull the turkey skin up under wings to hold it in shape and secure with skewers.

Tie legs together with string, making sure they are secured close to the body. Rub butter over breasts, legs, and wings, and season lightly with cinnamon, salt, and pepper.

Place turkey, breast down, in a roasting pan and cook for 20 minutes. Turn oven down to moderate (350°F/180°C/Gas 4) and cook for a further 3–3^1/2 hours. Check from time to time basting with pan juices, and covering with foil any parts which may be browning too quickly. Turn turkey onto its other side about a quarter of the way through cooking, then onto its back so that it cooks evenly. The turkey is cooked when juices run clear when a skewer is inserted through the thickest part of the thigh. Take care not to overcook.

Remove to a warm serving platter, discard string and skewers, and cover loosely with foil. Let rest 15–20 minutes while you make the gravy.

Cooking times for stuffed turkey:

- 6–8lb/3–4 kg turkey will take 3–3^1/2 hours and serve 8–10.
- 8–12 lb/4–6 kg turkey will take 3^1/2–4 hours and serve 10–14
- 12–16 lb/6–8 kg turkey will take 4–6 hours and serve 14–16

Pork and veal forcemeat

8 oz/250 g combination of minced (ground) pork and veal
2 oz/60 g fresh breadcrumbs
2 oz/60 g dried chestnuts, soaked overnight, or 4 oz/125 g fresh chestnuts, cooked and skinned
grated zest of 1 lemon
2 French shallots, finely chopped (see glossary)
2 tablespoons chopped fresh parsley
^{1}/2 teaspoon chopped fresh sage
1 small egg, beaten
salt and freshly ground black pepper

Mix all the ingredients together, seasoning with the salt and pepper.

Fruit and nut stuffing

3 oz/90 g prunes, halved and pitted
3 oz/90 g dried apricots, quartered
2 fl oz/60 ml Madeira or medium sherry
2 oz/60 g shelled walnuts, broken
2 oz/60 g blanched almonds, chopped
1 oz/30 g butter
1 onion, chopped
1 stick celery, chopped
1 tart green apple, peeled, cored, and chopped
1 pear, peeled, cored, and chopped
4 tablespoons chopped fresh parsley
1 tablespoon orange peel
1 teaspoon freshly chopped sage
^{1}/2 teaspoon fresh thyme leaves
^{1}/4 teaspoon nutmeg
^{1}/4 teaspoon cinnamon
1 teaspoon salt
freshly ground black pepper
3^1/2 oz/100 g day-old bread, cubed

Soak prunes and apricots overnight in a bowl with Madeira. Toast nuts in a moderate oven for 8–10 minutes. Melt butter in a heavy frying pan, and cook onion and celery until soft. Add apple and pear, and cook until softened. Remove pan from heat and stir in all remaining ingredients, except bread cubes. The stuffing can be prepared ahead up to this point.

Just before stuffing, add bread cubes, and macerated prunes and apricots. Combine well.

roast turkey, roasted vegetables, candied sweet potatoes, cranberry sauce

Candied sweet potatoes

6 medium sweet potatoes, preferably kumera
3¹/₂ oz/100 g brown sugar
juice and zest of 1 orange
cinnamon
2 oz/60 g butter

*P*reheat oven to 350°F (180°C/Gas 4). Cook sweet potatoes whole in boiling salted water until nearly tender. Drain, peel, and slice into ³/₄-in (2-cm) rounds. Arrange slices in a greased shallow ovenproof dish, layering with sugar, orange zest, and cinnamon. Pour in orange juice and dot with butter. Bake uncovered for 30–40 minutes, basting from time to time with the juices in the dish.

Green beans

*T*op and tail 2 lb/1 kg stringless green beans. Steam them until tender but firm.

Brussels sprouts and chestnuts

Streaky bacon, cut into strips and sautéed with the butter is a tasty addition.

1¹/₂ lb/750 g brussels sprouts, trimmed
8 oz/250 g canned whole chestnuts, or cooked and peeled
  fresh chestnuts
16 fl oz/500 ml chicken or beef stock
1¹/₂ oz/45 g butter
salt and freshly ground black pepper

*C*ook sprouts in boiling salted water for 6 minutes. Drain. Place chestnuts into a saucepan with stock and bring to a boil. Add sprouts, bring back to a boil, and simmer for 8–10 minutes or until sprouts are cooked but still crisp. Be careful not to let the chestnuts become mushy. Drain and toss in butter. Season to taste.

Roasted vegetables

The potatoes are best cooked in a separate pan in hot oil to ensure they are crisp. The onions can be placed around the turkey, if there's room, or added to the pan with the potatoes.

10–14 old potatoes, peeled and halved
10–14 medium onions, peeled
vegetable oil

*P*arboil potatoes and onions in boiling salted water for 5–8 minutes, drain, and dry on paper towels.
  Meanwhile, lightly film the bottom of a roasting pan with oil. About 1 hour before the turkey is due to be removed, place roasting pan in oven to heat up. When heated, place vegetables in a single layer in the dish. Baste with oil during cooking. If they need to crisp up, turn oven up after turkey has been removed.

Gravy

Make the stock while the turkey is cooking, and then make the gravy in the same pan in which the turkey was cooked.

turkey giblets
1 small onion
1 bay leaf
1 small carrot
1 celery stalk
48 fl oz/1.5 l water
2 tablespoons all-purpose (plain) flour
8 fl oz/250 ml dry white wine, optional
salt and pepper

While turkey is cooking, make stock: simmer giblets with onion, bay leaf, carrot, celery, and water until volume is reduced by half. Strain and refrigerate.

After removing turkey from the pan, skim excess fat from pan juices. Scatter flour over remaining pan juices and blend well over low heat, stirring with a fork for a minute or two to cook flour. Pour in 24 fl oz /750 ml stock, scraping up all the delicious residue stuck to the pan. Add wine, if using, and any of the juices from the carving platter. Simmer until the gravy begins to thicken. Season to taste. Strain through a sieve into a warmed gravy boat and serve piping hot.

green beans, brussel sprouts and chestnuts

Royal Christmas pudding

Christmas puddings can be made up to 6 months in advance and reheated on the day. This mixture will fill two 32-fl oz (1-l) pudding basins, each serving 6–8 or one 64-fl oz/2-l. You can use commercially prepared suet if you like. If citron is unavailable, substitute with more mixed peel. Don't forget to collect a few shiny coins to bury in the pudding. Serve with custard and/or hard sauce.

12 oz/375 g fresh, finely shredded beef suet
7¹/2 oz/225 g fresh white breadcrumbs
7¹/2 oz/225 g seedless raisins
7¹/2 oz/225 g sultanas (golden raisins)
7¹/2 oz/225 g currants
7¹/2 oz/225 g demerara or soft brown sugar
6 oz/175 g blanched ground almonds
3¹/2 oz/100 g plain (all-purpose) flour
1³/4 oz/50 g citron, diced (optional)
1³/4 oz/50 g glacée lemon peel, diced
1³/4 oz/50 g glacée orange peel, diced
7 fl oz/200 ml beer
3¹/2 fl oz/100 ml sherry
3¹/2 fl oz/100 ml brandy
4 55-g (large) eggs
1 teaspoon mixed spice
¹/4 teaspoon nutmeg
¹/4 teaspoon salt
finely grated zest of 1 orange

Combine all ingredients in a large bowl. You may like to ask family members and friends to come and stir the pudding, and make a wish as they stir. Cover with a cloth and allow to stand in a cool place for 12 hours.

Spoon mixture into one large or two smaller buttered pudding basins, pressing down well. Cover with buttered waxed (greaseproof) paper, pleated in the middle (this allows the pudding to expand as it cooks). Cover again with foil, also pleated in the middle, and tie both layers with string. At the top make a handle with the string, and knot securely—this will make it easier to lift the pudding in and out.

Set the pudding on a rack or upturned heatproof dish in a large pan of boiling water to reach halfway up the side of the pudding basin. Bring the water back to a boil after putting in the pudding, turn down to simmer, and put on the lid. Steam 8 hours for the large pudding or 4–5 hours for the smaller puddings. Top regularly with more boiling water. You will know the pudding is ready when it is firm to the finger and shrinks from the sides. Remove from water, take off waxed paper and foil, and re-cover with fresh layers. Store in a cool place.

On Christmas Day, boil the small puddings for 3 hours, the large one for 4 hours. Invert onto a warm platter to serve. Bury any coins as best you can, but wrap them first in waxed paper to save tainting the pudding.

Custard

1 vanilla bean, split in half lengthwise
32 fl oz/1 l milk
10 egg yolks
5 oz/150 g caster (superfine) sugar

Scrape seeds from vanilla bean into milk. Scald milk over medium heat and set aside.

In a bowl whisk egg yolks and sugar until light and thick. Pour warmed milk gradually onto yolks, whisking all the time. Wash the saucepan and return egg and milk mixture to it. Place over medium to low heat and cook until custard thickens, stirring continually. You will know it is ready when it coats the back of a spoon. Immediately remove from heat and pour through a sieve into a clean bowl. Serve warm or cold in a jug.

Hard sauce

Some people serve this rum or brandy butter instead of custard. But I like to have both with my pudding!

8 oz/250 g unsalted butter
5 oz/150 g caster (superfine) or 5 oz/150 g icing
    (powdered) sugar
1 teaspoon grated orange zest
1 teaspoon orange juice
about 2 fl oz/60 ml rum or brandy

Cream butter and sugar until soft and white, then beat in grated zest and juice until mixture is really pale, light, and fluffy. Add rum a little at a time, beating constantly so that the butter mixture doesn't curdle (add as much as the mixture will take). Pile into a bowl and refrigerate until hard.

Millie Sherman's Christmas cake

For many centuries fruit cakes have been associated with festivals and holidays. "Now the mirth comes with a cake full of plums," wrote 17th-century poet Robert Herrick of the English Christmas or "plum" cake. These cakes can be made up to year in advance, and really require a minimum of one month to mature. They are then decorated on the day (or the day before) serving—with marzipan and royal icing for a traditional Christmas cake, or with a soft white icing (see recipe opposite).

14 oz/400 g sultanas (golden raisins)
10¹/2 oz/300 g currants
7 oz/200 g dried apricots, diced
7 oz/200 g red glacé cherries, halved
3¹/2 oz/100 g mixed glacée peel
8 fl oz/250 ml Cognac
finely grated zest of 1 orange
finely grated zest of 1 lemon
8 oz/250 g pecans, coarsely chopped
butter, melted, for pan
8 oz/250 g unsalted butter, softened
8 oz/250 g brown sugar
5 55-g (large) eggs
1 teaspoon vanilla essence/extract
¹/2 teaspoon almond essence/extract
8 oz/250 g plain (all-purpose) flour
1 teaspoon baking powder
¹/2 teaspoon nutmeg
¹/2 teaspoon cinnamon
¹/2 teaspoon ground cloves

Place fruit and mixed peel into a large bowl. Pour over half the Cognac, mixing well to combine. Cover and set aside for several hours or overnight, stirring occasionally. Scatter the peel and nuts onto the fruit, and mix well.

Preheat oven to 275°F (140°C/Gas 1). Brush a 9-in (23-cm) tube pan with melted butter, line with double thickness of parchment (baking paper), and brush again with melted butter.

Cream softened unsalted butter with sugar until very light. Add eggs, one at a time, creaming well after each addition. Add vanilla and almond essences. Sift together flour and other dry ingredients. Add to the butter mixture alternately with the remaining Cognac, starting and ending with dry ingredients.

Spoon the batter onto fruit and nut mixture. Stir well to combine. Pour mixture into prepared pan, smoothing the top. Tap pan on counter a couple of times to settle mixture. Bake for 2¹/2–3 hours. Cool cake in the pan. When completely cold, turn out, remove paper, and re-wrap in foil. Store in a cool place until needed.

White icing

8 oz/250 g icing (powdered) sugar
3–4 tablespoons milk
a few drops vanilla essence/extract

Cream together all ingredients until smooth. Pour over Christmas cake, letting the icing drip over the sides.

Mince pies

These are delicious served warm, the lids slightly lifted and a little of the rum butter inserted underneath. Wicked! This recipe will make twelve 2¹/2-in (6.5-cm) pies.

For the pastry
8 oz/250 g all-purpose (plain) flour
2 teaspoons icing (powdered) sugar
pinch salt
5¹/2 oz/170 g unsalted butter, cut into small pieces
1 egg yolk, mixed with 1 tablespoon water
extra water, as required

For the filling
10 oz/300 g mincemeat
1 oz/30 g walnuts, chopped
2 tablespoons brandy
zest of 1 orange, finely chopped
¹/2 apple, grated, optional

icing (powdered) sugar, for dusting

Sift flour, sugar, and salt into a bowl. Make a well in the middle and put in butter and egg yolk mixed with water. With the fingers of one hand mix in butter and egg until mixture resembles coarse breadcrumbs. Add water a few drops at a time until mixture can be pressed firmly together. It should be soft but not sticky. Remove dough to a floured surface and knead a few times until soft and pliable. Press dough into a ball—it should look and feel like putty. Wrap in plastic or foil and refrigerate for 30 minutes.

Combine ingredients for filling and set aside. If the mincemeat is dry, add some grated apple.

Preheat the oven to 400°F (200°C/Gas 6).

Roll out chilled pastry, cut out circles to fit the size of your pie pans, allowing for an overlap. Line buttered pie pans with the circles. Spoon in filling. Cut out more circles, a little smaller than before. Cover the filling with these, and pinch the edges to seal. With a sharp knife, cut a cross in the top of each pie.

Bake until browned, about 15 minutes. Remove from oven, and cool slightly before removing from pans. When cold, dust with icing sugar.

Mincemeat

This makes a large quantity but it keeps well, refrigerated, for a very long time, and makes a lovely gift item. It is best made 2–3 months before Christmas.

1 lb/500 g beef suet, chopped
1 lb/500 g apples, peeled, cored, and roughly chopped
1 lb/500 g seedless raisins

8 oz/250 g mixed glacée peel
1 lb/500 g sultanas (golden raisins)
1 lb/500 g currants
12 oz/350 g brown sugar
5 fl oz/150 ml Cognac
2 teaspoons nutmeg
2 tablespoons slivered almonds
finely grated zest and juice of 1 orange and 1 lemon
extra Cognac, for topping up

*M*ix together the suet, apples, raisins, and peel. Pass through the large cutter of a mincer. Add the remaining ingredients and combine thoroughly. Pack into sterile glass jars, seal, and store in a cool, dark place. Top occasionally with more Cognac.

Gingerbread men

Follow the recipe for gingerbread in the jigsaw puzzle cake (see page 142), but halve the quantity. This will be enough to make 20 gingerbread men.

*P*reheat oven to 350°F (180°C/Gas 4). Roll out pastry onto a lightly floured board. Stamp out gingerbread man shapes with a cutter, and lift carefully onto lightly greased trays. Bake for about 15 minutes or until browned. Remove and let cool.

Decorate as you wish.

Christmas trees

Makes 10 large trees

11 oz/320 g unsalted butter, softened
6 oz/180 g caster (superfine) sugar
1/4 teaspoon salt
1 lb/500 g plain (all-purpose) flour
extra caster (superfine) sugar, for sprinkling

*P*reheat oven to 300°F (150°C/Gas 2). Cream together butter, sugar, and salt until pale and fluffy. Sift flour and knead into the creamed ingredients to give a rough dough. Place dough between sheets of non-stick parchment (baking paper) on the back of a baking tray and press out with palms of hands. Roll out to about 1/4 in (5 mm) thickness. Refrigerate for about 1/2 hour until hard.

Using a Christmas tree cutter, stamp out trees and place onto a greased baking tray. Bake for 20 minutes, then turn down heat to 200°F (100°C/Gas 1/8) and bake for 10–15 minutes until browned. Remove from oven and let cool.

When cool, sprinkle with extra caster sugar, and decorate with green and red ribbon and dragées.

gingerbread men, Christmas trees

A wedding at home

A wedding at home

Serves 10

**Crostini with Red Lentil Purée and Goat Cheese
or with Olive Paste and Capsicum**

~

Smoked Mackerel Pâté with Melba Toast

~

Roast Fillet of Beef with Mustard-Tarragon Butter

Baby Potatoes

Mesclun Salad with Green Chive Dressing

~

**Lime Icecream with Heart-Shaped Waffles
and Pistachio Nut Praline**

~

Wedding Cake

*M*ore intimate than at a reception room or hotel, being married at home is a very personal statement, not just of a couple's style but also of the way they envisage their future, setting the tone for their marriage and the life they will spend together.

There are many other advantages to being married in a home, whether it is your own, your family's, or a friend's. You know the terrain and feel comfortable in it; you have full control over the proceedings; you don't have to worry about booking or paying for reception rooms; and if you decide to have the ceremony at home as well, you don't need to book the church either.

A wedding is a celebration of the highest order, a rite of passage into a new and challenging stage of life. As such, arranging a wedding at home will require time, effort, and imagination. But take heart—daunting as it might seem at first, it can be a great success.

Planning the wedding

Start planning up to six months ahead. The celebrant, as well as the photographer, florist, musicians, and caterer—if you use their services—need to be advised as far as possible in advance. They are busy people and you may miss out on the person of your choice unless you book them well ahead.

If it's your wedding, clearly you will need help, but even if you are hosting the wedding of a family member or friend, you will require assistance and the nature of that assistance is up to you. The more guests, the more help you will need. It may mean extra hands in the kitchen, or you may want to call in a wedding-hire company who will organize everything from the champagne flutes through to the wedding cake. Whether you rely on the generosity of others or can afford to pay for professional help, sharing the load will help to ease inevitable tensions.

Let's start at the beginning with making lists. First, the engaged couple need to establish the guest list. This usually takes more time than anticipated because it not only involves a sometimes difficult selection process but also necessitates fixing a date,

Be imaginative in your decoration, and consider small details and special touches. If you have any garden statues, a bow will lend a festive air. At this wedding, a garland of ivy and roses circle the head of a wistful marble boy.

deciding the actual location inside or outside the house, determining how many people you can cater for in the home, the style of the wedding, and, very importantly, the budget. Traditionally, the main burden for the cost of a wedding fell on the bride's parents, but these days many families and the couple themselves may share the expense. It is sensible for financial limitations and divisions to be made clear by all parties right from the start. Weddings can be expensive affairs, and the budget, together with the guest list, should be firmly established before the details can be sorted out. The budget will be affected by all the other decisions you make, just as it will influence your choices.

When the guest list has been finalized, there are invitations to be considered. These need to specify who is marrying whom, and the date, time, and address of the home. If the ceremony is being performed elsewhere, additional details will have to be provided. You may also decide to ask only close friends and family for the ceremony, but more people to the reception. If that is the case, print some invitations for both the marriage ceremony and the reception, and others for the reception only. A reply date and return address should also be included, as well as the type of dress expected. Discussions will need to include the type of paper to be used, and whether the invitation is to be handwritten by someone specializing in calligraphy, printed by a professional printer, or perhaps constructed on a personal computer. A more personal tone can be established by handwriting the names, envelopes, and later, the place cards for the table.

If you don't hire professionals, you will have to do all the groundwork for the practical details: how many tables will fit into the chosen space? Do you want round or

For round tables, hire two tablecloths per table—the top cloth can be scalloped and give the table a very pretty look. Measure equal distances between each scallop and stitch the folds firmly with needle and thread. Cover with a bow in the ribbon of your choice.

rectangular ones? How many guests can be seated at each table? Will you put them inside or outside? Many people choose to seat guests at round tables and to set up a long rectangular table along one wall for the bridal party. If you are celebrating outdoors, it would be wise to erect a marquee or tent. Most hiring places will offer a choice of decorative lining and flooring—and, if it's a winter wedding, heating.

The trimmings

Decorating the inside of a marquee or the rooms in a house is time-consuming, but family and friends of all ages and levels of skill can do something to help in this area. Such activities often draw people closer together and create cherished memories.

When will the wedding be held? Different seasons require different approaches, for both practical and aesthetic reasons. The food and flowers you can obtain so easily in spring will be difficult to get hold of in the depths of winter. The marquee which is perfect for a summer wedding may be too lightweight for colder weather. Your house may suit an outdoor wedding better than an indoor one or vice versa, which will lead you to consider the seasons as well.

Tables, chairs, chair-covers, cloths, napkins, crockery, cutlery, and glasses will all

Tips for making your wedding at home a success

~ If there are guests from out-of-town, suggest a reasonably priced, charming guesthouse or hotel or motel where they can stay. Other relatives may offer to board guests. If so, organize this well ahead.

~ Ask a gregarious (and gracious) family member or friend to greet guests either at the front door or gate.

~ Make sure you have set aside a room for guests' coats, bags, and the like.

~ Cutting the wedding cake often precedes the speeches—it can then be discreetly distributed by the people waiting tables.

~ Cutting the wedding cake is something to be done with care. Entrust the task to someone responsible—perhaps the person who made it.

~ Keep any speeches as short as possible— this is meant to be a celebration. A microphone may be necessary—make sure equipment is positioned to give an even distribution of sound.

~ Half-fill clean plastic tubs with ice and use to store champagne and wine in bulk, or use the bathtub.

have to be organized. These will probably need to be hired, and all those people involved in the wedding plans may wish to view together a number of available options before deciding.

Work out your seating plan well before the reception. The most important table is obviously the bridal one. Traditionally, the bride sits on the bridegroom's left; next to the bride is her father; then the bridegroom's mother and best man. Next to the bridegroom is the bride's mother, his father, then the chief bridesmaid. Other bridesmaids or groomsmen are then seated after that.

A table for the wedding cake will need to be provided, and also one for the signing of the register if the ceremony is being held at home. You may also like to set aside a separate room for photography. It's a good idea to do the more formal shots prior to the arrival of guests, then the remaining pictures can be more spontaneous. The majority of receptions would also require an area for dancing with a hard, smooth but non-slip surface.

Most people like to call on a florist for the bridal bouquet and the bridesmaid's flowers. If you want to place floral arrangements in the middle of the tables, or perhaps a garland over a doorway, a professional's touch will ensure that the flowers are both fresh and stunning. For those who wish to do it themselves, the chapter on Floral Decoration (page 32) will provide some basic guidelines. Work out your decorating scheme and the bridal parties' clothes before finalizing the flowers so that they complement.

The music played prior to the ceremony and then at the reception is a very personal choice. It may be classical or contemporary, prerecorded on CD or cassette, or performed live by musicians, perhaps a pianist or small ensemble, or an organist.

When planning the menu, keep it simple but delicious. Three courses is ample, especially if followed by coffee and wedding cake. Choose dishes for the first course and dessert that can be prepared ahead. It's difficult to avoid any last-minute cooking at a sit-down dinner, so try to keep this to a minimum with the main course, and organize people to help—someone you can rely on to do the cooking, another to help plate the food, and others to take the hot main course to the tables.

This menu

The wedding featured in this chapter was a late summer celebration held at sunset for 50 people. Guests were invited for the wedding ceremony at 5 pm sharp, then offered champagne and crostini once the ceremony had been conducted. After a glass or two of champagne, guests were encouraged to sit down at the tables, guided by name cards tucked into the napkins. The mackerel pâté in its lime container was removed from the refrigerator during the ceremony and plated with the melba toast and a sprig of

Wine suggestions

~ With the crostini: a rich, complex, dry-style vintage Champagne.

~ With the pâté: a German spatlese or kabinett-style Riesling from the Mosel, or a mature Australian riesling.

~ With the scotch fillet: a full-bodied cabernet-based red, ideally a Bordeaux from the Médoc, a cabernet sauvignon from California or Australia, or a "Super Tuscan" vino da tavola from Italy.

~ With dessert: an intense, youthful sweet white such as a beerenauslese riesling from the Rheingau, or a late-harvest chenin blanc from Vouvray or Anjou.

watercress. It was served as soon as all guests were seated.

The scotch fillets were put into the oven halfway through the ceremony and then left to rest while the first course was being eaten. The salads, already prepared and on their platters or in their bowls, were then dressed and the potatoes cooked through and tossed in the melted butter.

While the main course was being eaten, the waffles were plated and the icecream and praline only added at the last minute.

With the exception of the wedding cake and salad dressing, the recipes in this menu serve 10 people, which means you can easily multiply by 5 or 8 or 10 to work out quantities for guests. (The wedding cake serves 25 as a dessert, or 45–50 as an accompaniment to coffee—see recipe on page 199.)

Crostini

Allow 3-4 crostini per person; a ficelle will give you about 30–40 slices, depending on its length. They are quick nibbles to be served with champagne as guests arrive. Encourage your guests to be seated after one glass of champagne.

1–2 ficelle (thin French bread stick), cut diagonally into
    thin slices
1–2 cut cloves garlic
extra virgin olive oil

P reheat oven to 400°F (200°C/Gas 6). Toast bread in oven for 5-10 minutes or until golden. Remove from oven and, whilst still hot, rub each slice with a cut clove of garlic. Lightly brush or spray each slice with olive oil. Store in air-tight containers.

Red lentil purée with goat cheese

This recipe makes enough for 2–3 ficelle. Store extra purée in an air-tight in the refrigerator.

7 oz/200 g red lentils
4 cups (32 fl oz/1 l) water
flaky sea salt and freshly ground pepper
juice of 1/2 lemon
1–2 cloves garlic, crushed
3 fl oz/80 ml virgin olive oil
2–3 medium fresh goat cheeses, thinly sliced

S oak lentils for 2–3 hours in water to cover. Scoop off any that rise to the surface. Drain well, washing under cold running water. Place in a large saucepan and cover with 4 cups water. Bring to a boil and let simmer gently, about 5–10 minutes, until soft but still al dente. Strain. Whilst still warm, season with salt, pepper, lemon juice, garlic (to taste), and olive oil. Let cool.

Spoon a little of the red lentil mixture onto the crostini and top with goat cheese.

crostini

Olive paste and capsicum

1 red capsicum (bell pepper)
1 yellow capsicum (bell pepper)
1 6-oz/185-g jar good-quality black olive paste

Roast capsicums following the method on page 163. When cool, slice into thin strips, then cut into small pieces.

Spread the crostini with a little olive paste. Place one small yellow and one small red strip overlapping on top of each crostini.

Smoked mackerel pâté

Allow about 1 oz (30 g) pâté for each person; this makes enough for 10 people. Serve with melba toast (see recipe overleaf). You can use some of the leftover lime juice for the lime icecream (see page 198).

12 oz/375 g smoked mackerel, off the bone (4 small or
   3 large fillets)

2 oz/60 g unsalted butter, softened
paprika
freshly ground black pepper
squeeze lime juice
2 fl oz/60 ml thickened or whipping cream
10 limes, for containers
watercress, for garnish

Process all ingredients except cream, limes, and watercress in a food processor until well blended. Add cream and process until well combined.

Wash limes well. Cut a good lid off their tops, and slice across their bottoms so they sit flat. Squeeze out the juice into a bowl by rotating a small teaspoon in the lime flesh; reserve juice. With a small sharp knife, scrape out remaining flesh from the pith, to leave a neat container.

Spoon the pâté into limes and serve accompanied by melba toast. Garnish plates with watercress.

roast fillet of beef with mustard-tarragon butter, baby potatoes

Melba toast

Allow 2 pieces of toast per person.

Slice 3–4 rosette (Italian bread rolls) very finely with a serrated knife. Alternatively, use a loaf of white bread and trim off the crusts. (Slicing is easiest when the bread is partially frozen.)

Place slices on a baking sheet and bake in an oven pre-heated to 350°F (180°C/Gas 4), or grill (broil) until pale golden, watching carefully. Store in air-tight containers.

Roast fillet of beef with mustard–tarragon butter

Allow about 5–7 oz/150–200 g meat for each person. Serve with baby potatoes and bowls of mesclun salad (see recipes opposite).

1 long scotch fillet, about 4 lb/2 kg, trimmed of all fat
   and membranes
freshly ground black pepper
flaky sea salt
2¹/₂ oz/75 g butter

Tie fillet together at intervals with string to ensure it keeps a good shape. Season with pepper and salt. Heat butter in a large pan and sear meat on all sides until brown. (You can prepare the dish ahead up to this point.)

Preheat oven to 425°F (220°C/Gas 7). Cook fillet for 30–40 minutes. Press meat with your fingers to check for "doneness"—it should give a little. If you want it well done, wait until there is no resistance in the meat. (If you remain unsure, slice a piece off and have a look.) Let rest, wrapped in foil, for 5–10 minutes in a warm place while you finish the potatoes.

Cut string off meat and slice thickly into about 10 slices. Arrange on warm serving platters and serve with the mustard–tarragon butter.

Mustard–tarragon butter

4 oz/125 g butter, softened
1 tablespoon Dijon mustard
1¹/₂ tablespoons dried tarragon

Cream butter with mustard and tarragon. Form into a roll about 1 inch (2.5 cm) in diameter, using foil to help shape it. Wrap well and chill until firm. Cut into 10 slices and serve a slice with each portion of beef.

Baby potatoes

Allow about 3 potatoes per person.

2 lb/1 kg baby potatoes
4 oz/125 g butter, melted

Steam or cook potatoes in boiling salted water. (You can parcook the potatoes ahead, then finish the cooking while the meat is resting.)

Cut each potato in half and toss in melted butter.

Mesclun salad with green chive dressing

Mesclun is the French name for mixed baby salad leaves (oak leaf, radicchio, lamb's tongue, mizuna, mustard leaves, and baby spinach, to name a few). These are now readily available pre-mixed from specialty shops and supermarkets, but you can also make your own mix. Allow a good handful per person. For 10 people, you will need 1 lb/500 g. Wash your choice of leaves and dry well. Toss with green chive dressing (see recipe below).

Green chive dressing

This should dress 4 large bowls of salad or enough for about 40 people.

1 bunch chives, washed and chopped finely
5 fl oz/150 ml white wine vinegar
good pinch flaky sea salt
16 fl oz/500 ml olive oil

Process chives, vinegar, and sea salt in a blender or food processor until well combined, then drizzle in olive oil.

lime icecream with heart-shaped waffles and pistachio nut praline

Lime icecream with heart-shaped waffles and pistachio nut praline

If you use the juice from the limes that were scooped out to make containers for the smoked mackerel pâté (see page 195), you will only need 2 limes for the icecream, instead of 4.

6 egg yolks
7¹/₂ oz/225 g caster (superfine) sugar

juice of 4 large limes, strained
zest of 2 limes, finely grated
10 fl oz/300 ml cream

Beat yolks and sugar in a mixing bowl until thick and creamy. Gradually beat in lime juice and zest.

In another bowl, whip cream lightly and fold into egg mixture. Freeze in an icecream maker, following manufacturer's instructions. Spoon into plastic trays, cover with a lid, and freeze. Remove from freezer 10–15 minutes before serving.

Heart-shaped waffles

*If you don't have a heart-shaped waffle iron, you can use an
ordinary one. The recipe makes 20 waffles, allow 2 per person.*

8 oz/250 g plain (all-purpose) flour
14 fl oz/400 ml buttermilk
1/2 teaspoon baking powder
3 tablespoons sugar
2 eggs
1 teaspoon vanilla essence/extract
2 1/2 oz/75 g butter, melted and cooled
vegetable oil

*P*rocess all ingredients except butter and oil in a blender
or food processor until well combined. Add melted
butter and blend again.

Lightly brush waffle iron with oil. Heat it, then cook the
waffles. (Don't worry if the first few aren't perfect.)

Pistachio nut praline

1 teaspoon vegetable oil
6 oz/185 g caster (superfine) sugar
2 fl oz/60 ml water
4 oz/125 g unsalted pistachio nuts, roughly chopped

*L*ightly oil a small baking sheet. Bring sugar and water
slowly to a boil in a heavy saucepan, stirring to dissolve. Let simmer until it turns a golden caramel. Pour in
nuts, and shake to combine well. Pour onto baking sheet
and let cool until hard and brittle.

Roughly chop the praline with a knife on a chopping
board and sprinkle a little over each scoop of icecream.

Wedding cake

*A no-fuss cake with great results. The method is straightforward and
achievable at home. Only one rosette is required for the piping,
which, after a little practice, is also easy to do.*

*This is a European-style wedding cake, similar in taste and tex-
ture to a Madeira cake. Unlike a fruit cake, it can also be served as
dessert (accompanied with poached fruit or a fruit sauce and cream).
As a dessert, it will serve 25 or more. If served with coffee, it will
serve 45–50.*

The top layer can be frozen and kept for later.

*For both the cake and the buttercream, all ingredients should be
at room temperature before you start.*

wedding cake

Lemon buttercake

1 lb 2oz/550 g unsalted butter
2 lb/900 g caster (superfine) sugar
10 55-g (large) eggs
5 55-g (large) eggs, separated
1¹/2 lb/700g plain (all-purpose) flour
5 oz/150 g cornflour (cornstarch)
2 tablespoons baking powder
1 teaspoon salt
18 fl oz/550 ml milk
2 teaspoons pure lemon essence/extract
finely grated zest of 2 lemons

*B*utter and flour a 9-in (23-cm) round cake pan and a 12-in (30-cm) round cake pan, each no deeper than 2 in (5 cm). Preheat oven to 325°F (160°C/Gas 3).

Cream butter, then slowly add sugar, creaming well after each addition. Add whole eggs plus 5 yolks, three at a time, creaming until each addition is incorporated and batter is smooth. On lowest speed of mixer, start adding sifted dry ingredients alternating with milk, starting and ending with dry ingredients. Beat in lemon essence and grated zest. (If your mixer is too small for the amount specified, make two batches; keep one half refrigerated while preparing the second half. Then mix both halves together by hand in a large basin.)

In a separate bowl, whisk 5 egg whites to a softly mounding snow, then fold into batter. Divide mixture and fill each cake pan until about two-thirds full.

Bake small cake for 50–60 minutes, and large cake for 65–75 minutes. Cakes should be golden on top and pull away slightly from the sides. Remove from oven, and leave in pans for 10 minutes. Turn out onto cooling racks. Set aside to cool.

Light lemon buttercream

6 egg whites
11 ¹/2 oz/350 g caster (superfine) sugar
1 ¹/2 lb/750 g unsalted butter
2 tablespoons pure lemon essence/extract

*P*lace egg whites and sugar in a basin set over a saucepan of simmering water. The water should not touch the bottom of the basin. Using a hand-held mixer, whisk mixture for 7–10 minutes until it is firm and has tripled in size. Remove from heat, set basin in a container with a few ice cubes, and continue whisking until meringue is completely cool.

In another bowl, cream butter until light and fluffy, then add meringue to butter in large spoonsful, creaming well after each addition. Lastly, add lemon essence.

Assembling the cake
You will need four decorative pillars, about 6 ins (15 cm) high, with a base and top; a piping bag with rosette tube; and a 9-in (23-cm) cake board and a 15-in (38-cm) cake board, both covered in silver paper. All of these are available from a cake decorating store. You will also need 4 plastic drinking straws.

First, place the cakes on the boards and, using a metal spatula, cover each one in a thin layer of buttercream. Place both cakes in the refrigerator for about 20 minutes.

Starting with the smaller cake, spread over a thicker layer of buttercream. Start with the top of the cake, spreading the cream right to the sides, then smooth the sides with more buttercream. Return cake to refrigerator. Repeat for the larger cake. Refrigerate again for 20 minutes to firm the buttercream.

You can now use your imagination to decorate both cakes, or use the photograph as a model. We used small piped rosettes in a scallop design on the sides of the cake and again around the bottom and top edges of cakes. Keep refrigerated until needed.

To complete, measure the depth of the bottom cake and cut two lengths from each straw to give you eight pieces the same depth as the cake. Press straws into top of cake 3¹/2 in (9 cm) from edge, spacing them evenly in a circle to fit the pillar base. Place bottom base on top of straws, fit pillars in slots. Place top base on pillars and place cake on top of that. Arrange flowers as you wish. It is a good idea to assemble the wedding cake on the table on which it is to be displayed, so as to avoid accidents.

wedding cake

Acknowledgements

Margaret Connolly and Jamie Grant for their support

Jerry and Bob Rogers for lending their lovely house

John Duffecy for lending us his Mediterranean backyard

Jan Berry for her nifty styling and her joyful breakfast room

André Martin for all his fabulous photography

Millie Sherman for all her ideas and fabulous cakes

Cherise Koch for her enthusiasm and stylish way with food

Christine Falvey for her marvellous way with words

Huon Hooke for his guidelines on wine

Jenny Ferguson for lending her dining room and time and ideas

Katie Highfield for lending her balcony and time and ideas

Marita Blood for lending her wonderful kitchen

Rosemary Penman for always being helpful

Karen Uren for her Harvo Loaf

Suzie Clemo for her fabulous lime ice-cream recipe

Ralph Potter, executive chef, Darley's restaurant at Lilianfels, Katoomba Australia for his recipe ideas

Kim's, Toowoon Bay Australia for the Dunkirk Bread recipe

Bill and Toula Langas of Myahgah Mews Deli

Blast!, The Rocks, Sydney Australia for their zany napkins

Peach Panfili of Peach 'n Lavish, Mosman, Sydney Australia for her fabulous flowers and arrangements

Pages Hire Centre, Chatswood, Sydney Australia— thanks to Lloyd Jansson and staff for the wedding tables, chairs, and cloths

Jacinta Preston at Miscellanea, Cremorne Point , Sydney Australia for her gorgeous cherub napkins

Hardy Brothers, Double Bay, Sydney Australia for their silver trays

Accoutrement, Mosman, Sydney Australia for lots of props

Sandy de Beyer for her props and ribbons.

Jane Curry, Deborah Nixon, Catherine Martin, and Kirsten Tilgals, at Lansdowne

The Lord Wedgwood of Barlaston

Carole Lewis, Fiona Lingard, and staff of Wedgwood, Castle Hill, Sydney Australia

Waterford Wedgwood designs

A long, late breakfast, pages 36-47—*Countryware Dinnerware (Wedgwood); Sheila Tumbler, Lismore Jug (Waterford).*

A gourmet barbecue, pages 48-61—*Cantata Dinnerware, Plain White Traditional Dinnerware (Wedgwood); Sheila Tumbler (Waterford); Clara Water/Pilsener (Marquis).*

A picnic in the garden, pages 62-71:—*Osborne Dinnerware (Wedgwood); Curraghmore Tumblers (Waterford).*

A winter lunch in the kitchen, pages 72-79—*Candlelight White Dinnerware (Wedgwood); Kathleen Jug & Tall Hock (Waterford).*

The delights of afternoon tea, pages 80-91—*Wild Strawberry Dinnerware, Strawberry & Vine white Dinnerware (Wedgwood); Hanover Gold Glass, Calais Vase, Palladia Bowl (Marquis).*

An impromptu meal from the pantry, pages 92-101—*Plain White Traditional Dinnerware (Wedgwood); Lismore Glasses (Waterford).*

A dinner party, pages 102-111—*Queen's Plain Dinnerware (Wedgwood); Lismore Tall Hock, Alana Footed Compote (Waterford).*

A romantic dinner for two, pages 112-121—*Strawberry & Vine Dinnerware (Wedgwood); Ice Bucket, Kildare diamond cut Glasses, Lismore Candlesticks, Footed Turnover Bowl, Sheila flat cut Glasses (Waterford).*

A midsummer night's theme, pages 122-133—*Chippendale Dinnerware (Wedgwood); Curraghmore Tall Hock (Waterford).*

A child's birthday party, pages 134-147—*Peter Rabbit China, Plain White Traditional Plate (Wedgwood).*

A buffet, pages 148-157—*Runnymede Dark Blue Dinnerware (Wedgwood); Colleen Goblet (Waterford).*

Cocktail parties for six or sixty, pages 158-171—*Cavendish Dinnerware (Wedgwood); Punch Bowl, Sheila Glasses (Waterford).*

A festive Christmas, pages 172-187—*Colorado Dinnerware (Wedgwood); Sheila Glasses, Ships Decanter (Waterford).*

A wedding at home, pages 188-201—*California Dinnerware (Wedgwood); Curraghmore Glasses (Waterford).*

Glossary

Antipasto—the Italian version of hors d'oeuvre or appetizers served either hot or cold on individual plates or from a platter.

Aspic or mini-cutters—tiny cutters (1/2–3/4in/12–20mm) made from tinned steel for cutting decorative shapes.

Baba ghannouj—a Middle Eastern dip made from eggplant (aubergine) which has been roasted or held over a flame with its skin on, and the flesh mashed and mixed with various seasonings and olive oil.

Breadcrumbs—for fresh breadcrumbs, trim day-old bread of crusts and rub through a wire sieve or process in food processor. For dried breadcrumbs, use trimmed bread which has been dried out in the oven, then process to very fine crumbs in the food processor or blender.

Cachous—small decorative balls used for cakes and cookies. Made from sugar, they are silver, gold, bright pink, and green.

Chafing dish—a copper pan or oval dish used for warming food.

Chicken galantine—a glantine is a boned bird (chicken, duck, turkey) filled with forcemeat (stuffing) mixture. It is wrapped and tied into a sausage shape and poached in broth, cooled, and served in its own aspic.

Chartreuse—a liqueur made originally by French monks in the French Alps at Chartreuse. It is either green or yellow.

Cheeses. *Gorgonzola*—a soft, moist cheese that is cream with blue-green veins. Of Italian origin, this is one of the world's great blue cheeses. *Goat cheese*—any cheese made from goat's milk rather than cow's milk. There are hundreds of varieties, most of which are soft with either a bloomy rind, smeared surface or covered in ash. Their shapes and sizes vary from logs to pyramids, balls and discs. In the menu for A Wedding at Home, a soft, ash-covered variety would be ideal. *Fetta*—an uncooked, soft white cheese which is "pickled" in brine to give it its characteristic salty taste. *Ricotta*—a mild, sweet soft white cheese that is made from the whey of the milk. The type referred to in this book is "tipo dolce" which is unsalted and unripened.

Citron—a large lemon-shaped citrus which has a tough, thick skin covering a very thick skin or pith. The skin (peel) is fragrant and is frequently candied.

Couscous—these tiny granules are made from semolina grains. The semolina is moistened and coated with flour. The word can refer to both the complete dish and the granules of semolina from which is it made. In Morocco, the dish is the crowning glory of Moroccan cuisine.

Cracked wheat (bulgur/burghul)—hulled wheat which is steamed until partly cooked, then dried and cracked or crushed into fine and coarse grades. It is a very important grain throughout the Middle East.

Cream of tartar—purified, crystallized potassium bi-tartrate which can be used with bicarbonate of soda to make baking powder. Often added to egg whites as a stabilizer.

Cream—single (light) or fresh pouring cream is the most com-monly used cream; it has a fairly low fat content that varies from country to country (from 18% to 35%). Double cream has a higher fat content and a thicker texture. Thickened cream is cream with a small amount of gelatine added to stabilize and thicken it; it holds well when whipped, and has a longer storage life than single cream. Whipping cream is available in some countries; it has a medium fat content. When purchasing cream for whipping, the optimum fat content is 35% which allows it to be whipped to double its volume.

Crème fraîche—cream treated with a special culture which helps it to stay fresher longer and gives it a delicious tang.

Crostini—oval-shaped toasted bread that has been rubbed with a cut garlic clove and drizzled with olive oil; Italian in origin.

Demerara (raw sugar)—a pale brown sugar distinguished by its larger crystal size and taste.

Focaccia—a rectangular or disc-shaped bread of peasant origin that is very popular in Italy and also known in some parts of southern France. It can be soft or crisp, plain or topped, thick or thin.

Gazpacho—a cold soup, originally made by the Arabs from bread, water, olive oil and vinegar. It was embellished by the Andalusians with tomatoes and capsicums and is one of the great summer soups.

Guacamole—a green dip of Mexican origin. The main ingredient is avocado, seasoned with chili, lemon juice and garlic.

Hummus—a spread or dip made from cooked, pureed chickpeas and tahini (ground sesame seeds), seasoned with garlic, lemon juice, and olive oil. Very popular in the Middle East.

Knock down—a step in bread making and yeast cookery in which the dough is "knocked back" after the first rising (proving) to expel excess carbon dioxide. Turn the risen (proved) dough out onto the bench, punch your fist in the middle and knead several times. Shape as required and leave to rise (or prove) again. Check the dough by quickly pressing two fingers into the top—if the dent remains, the dough is ready.

Kuzu—powdered lumpy starchy material from the tuberous root of the Asian kuzu vine. Similar to tapioca, it is used for thickening sauces and has twice the thickening power of arrowroot.

Mascarpone—a fresh unripened Italian triple cream cheese. It has a rich sweet taste and is slightly acidic.

Mincemeat—a preserve made of minced dried fruits and spices and laced with brandy or rum. Very traditional in Britain, where it is used to fill small sweet pies at Christmas. In the past, minced meats and suet were also used.

Mole—a traditional Mexican sauce which includes unsweetened-chocolate and chili.

Moussaka—a traditional Mediterranean dish made with eggplant (aubergine), minced (ground) lamb or beef and bechamel sauce enhanced with yogurt, cheese, and beaten egg.

Olives—there are hundreds of varieties of olives. One of the most popular is the kalamata which comes from Kalamata in the Greek

Peloponnesus. These are black or purple-black with an elongated shape and taste mild and fruity. The difference between green and black olives is merely a matter of ripeness. Prepared olives may be green, turning color (rosy, violet, brown) or ripening (darkened or natural black). Pimento-stuffed olives are the Spanish green manzanillas which have been pitted and then stuffed with red capsicum. Green jumbos are large and extra large green olives.

Onions—there is much confusion regarding the naming of the many different varieties of onions, and the same names in different countries can refer to different types. *Spring onions* (alium cepa) are those with small white bulbs, which have the same concentric circles as a mature onion but are pulled when the tops are still quite green. They are at a more advanced stage than the green onion or scallion. The *green onion* or *scallion* is long and slender with a white, slim bulb and dark green top. This is sometimes also called a *shallot*. The *red onion* is frequently called a *Spanish onion* or a *purple onion*. It is medium-large and red-purple with concentric circles. It has a delicious mild taste and is good in salads.

Orange blossom water—extracted from orange blossoms by steam distillation, this is an aromatic liquid with a subtle orange taste. Is used extensively in Moroccan cooking. Similarly, rosewater is an essence distilled from fragrant rose petals and used extensively in Middle Eastern cooking.

Pancetta—cured pork belly of Italian origin. Bacon can be substituted but is not as tasty.

Pappadums—thin crisp wafers made from lentil, potato, or rice flour that accompany many Indian dishes.

Penne—commercially made pasta which is shaped like a quill and cut diagonally at each end. The ridged variety is called penne rigate.

Petits fours—these tiny mouthfuls are served with coffee after a meal. They may be anything from madeleines, palmiers, tuiles, and truffles to candied peel, tiny meringues or macaroons, and shortbread biscuits. Keep them small.

Piping bag—you can make a piping cone, horn, or cornet from parchment, sulfurized paper, or wax paper. (1) Cut a triangle of paper. (2) With your thumbs and forefingers, hold each end of the triangle and roll one end into the triangle to form a loose cone. (3) With your thumbs inside and fingers outside, hold onto the open end of the cone at the seam. (4) Slide the paper between your fingers to tighten the cone into a sharper point. (5) Holding the cone tightly to avoid unrolling, fold the ends inside to hold them secure. (6) Fill the cone with mixture and squeeze gently on the cone to force mixture out of the point.

Polenta (cornmeal)—yellow-white granular flour made from corn or maize. It is graded according to texture, and can be fine, medium, or coarsely ground. In northern Italy, polenta is a staple food. It can be served soft or grilled (broiled).

Porcini—a wild mushroom (boletus edulis) which grows in Europe. In Italy, it is colloquially referred to as "porcini" because the specimens look like fat little pigs.

Preserved ginger—the peeled root of the ginger plant which has been preserved in sugar syrup; usually eaten as a sweetmeat or added to various desserts.

Prove—means "to rise", a step used in bread making and yeast cookery. See "knock down" for details.

Quinoa—referred to as the "mother grain" by the Incas of South America, this is a small grain resembling millet. When cooked, the tiny pellets swell and become translucent.

Rocket—also known as arugola, rucola, and roquet, this is a nutty salad green which can also taste quite peppery.

Salmon roe—bright orange, large-grained eggs from the female fish. All roe is sometimes mistakenly referred to as caviar.

Salt cod—also known as bacalhau and morue, these are salted, dried fillets of the North Atlantic cod which need soaking in frequent changes of water for up to 24 hours before using.

Sambal—accompaniments to curry meals which lend varying tastes and textures. They can be either cooling (cucumber sambal) or fiery (sambal oelek).

Sashimi tuna—very fine slices of tuna, best taken from the yellow fin tuna. The fish must be eaten very fresh, ideally on the day it is caught and killed in a specific way. Marbled flesh (with white lines of fat permeating the meat) is much prized.

Semolina—coarsely milled grains of wheat obtained when bran, wheat germ, and endosperm are separated. Semolina comes from the first milling of the endosperm. It can be bought fine, medium, or coarse ground.

Spatchcock—baby chickens, about six weeks old, weighing about 1 lb (500 g). Also known as poussin.

Suet—firm, white fat around the kidney of lamb or beef. Use beef suet in cooking. It can be purchased solid from the butcher or in packet form, grated with a little flour added, ready for use.

Tabbouli—this is a very popular Middle Eastern salad or side dish made from cracked wheat (bulgur), chopped flat-leaf parsley and mint, diced onions and tomatoes, lemon juice and olive oil.

Tahini—also known as tahina, a Middle Eastern paste made from ground toasted sesame seeds.

Tear-drop tomatoes—tiny yellow tomatoes about 1 in (2.5 cm) in length which are shaped like tears or pears.

Tortillas—national bread of Mexico. These thin flat round cakes made with cornmeal are cooked on a griddle without browning. Tortilla is also the Spanish name for omelette.

Turkey buffe—the upright breast of the turkey, sold with the carcass attached.

Vinegar—an acid liquid obtained from different fruits and grains after fermentation takes place. White or distilled vinegar is most often used for pickling due to its sharpness. The delicious wine vinegars can be made from either white or red wines. Apple cider vinegar is strong and distinctive, and is sharper than wine vinegar. It is also used for pickling.

Zuccotto—a dome-shaped Italian dessert. The bowl is lined with fingers of moistened madeira cake.

Zuppa inglese—an Italian dessert with a soupy-consistency made with layers of cake and custard cream, laced with rum.

Index

First published in the United Kingdom in 1994 by
Cassell
Villiers House
41/47 Strand
London WC2N 5JE

by arrangement with Lansdowne Publishing Pty Ltd, Australia

Additional text:
Christine Falvey: A Guide to Modern Etiquette, Hints for Serving and Eating,
The Table, The Art of Napkin Folding
Huon Hooke: Choosing and Serving Wine, wine suggestions throughout
Peach Panfili: Floral Decoration

British Library Cataloguing-in-Publication Data
A catalogue record for this book is available from the British Library

ISBN 0-304-34481-8

Printed in Singapore by Kyodo Printing Co (S'pore) Pte Ltd